DIVORCE GUIDE FOR ILLINOIS

DIVORCE GUIDE FOR ILLINOIS

Jennifer A. Carsen

Self-Counsel Press Inc.
(a subsidiary of)
International Self-Counsel Press Ltd.
USA   Canada

National Library of Canada Cataloguing in Publication

Carsen, Jennifer A.
   Divorce guide for Illinois/Jennifer A. Carsen.

(Self-counsel legal series)
ISBN 1-55180-447-6

   1. Divorce—Law and legislation—Illinois—Popular works.
2. Divorce suits—Illinois—Popular works. I. Title. II. Series.
KFI1300.Z9C37 2003   346.77301'66   C2003-905452-7

Self-Counsel Press Inc.
(a subsidiary of)
International Self-Counsel Press Ltd.

1704 N. State Street	1481 Charlotte Road
Bellingham, WA 98225	North Vancouver, BC V7J 1H1
USA	Canada

CONTENTS

Samples

NOTICE TO READERS

INTRODUCTION

This book, written by a lawyer, is directed toward filling the general public's need for information. Every citizen should know his or her rights and know how to use the courts to enforce these rights. This book is just one in the Self-Counsel Legal Series.

The directions and explanations in this book are reduced to a simple step-by-step process to help you understand the divorce proceedings.

You can obtain your own divorce, as it is the right of every citizen to take his or her own case to court. It will require time and energy on your part, but the ultimate objective of this book is to make lack of money no obstacle to obtaining a divorce.

However, there are some situations in which this book cannot help you. In these cases, *consultation with an attorney is mandatory*. Specifically, if your divorce is contested *for any reason whatsoever*, you will require an attorney. If you cannot afford an attorney, you should consult your local legal aid office. Contact information is provided in this book.

1

CAN YOU DO YOUR OWN DIVORCE?

1. DO YOU NEED A DIVORCE ATTORNEY?

This book explains the process for an *uncontested* divorce — meaning that you and your spouse are able to resolve, on your own, issues pertaining to child custody and support, maintenance (formerly called *alimony*), and property division. If this is your situation, you should be able to proceed on your own, without the help of an attorney.

However, there are some circumstances in which you should strongly consider hiring a divorce attorney:

(a) *If you have no idea where your spouse is:* As is explained later in the book (see Chapter 5, section **2.2**), divorce usually involves "serving" certain papers on your spouse. If you don't know where he or she is living, you may need a lawyer to help you out. While this book does explain the process for divorcing an absent spouse, you shouldn't hesitate to seek professional counsel if you are at all uncertain or confused.

(b) *If your spouse is abusive to you or your children:* Divorce proceedings may set off a volatile spouse. While this is something that you don't have much control over, a divorce attorney can act as an intermediary so that you and your spouse don't have as much direct contact throughout the divorce process. An attorney can also give you advice about the best way to protect yourself, your children, and your assets. If you have any reason to fear for your safety, hire an attorney — for your sake and your children's.

(c) *If you and your spouse cannot deal with one another:* The divorce process requires a great deal of "divvying up" — money, assets (e.g., cars and houses), and shared child custody arrangements. If you and your spouse are able to rationally discuss and mutually resolve these issues, your divorce will probably be fairly straightforward. But if you find you cannot even be in the same room with one another, it will be very difficult to come to any kind of agreement. Things may progress easier and faster if you have an attorney. While it's certainly not impossible to represent yourself in a contentious divorce, it's much more difficult — and you don't want to find yourself in the position of giving up things that are important to you just for the sake of getting things over with. An attorney is someone who will go to bat for you.

(d) *If you and your spouse cannot come to an agreement on a critical issue:* Even if you and your spouse get along, if you disagree about the terms of your divorce, or about the divorce itself, it is called a *contested* divorce. Contested divorces are generally more expensive than uncontested divorces and take longer. If your divorce is contested for any reason, see a lawyer so that you can protect your rights.

If you decide to hire an attorney, make sure you get some kind of cost estimate beforehand. Don't be shy about this. You do not want to wind up in over your head financially, especially during the stress of a divorce. Most attorneys will be happy to tell you how their fee structures work and about how much time your divorce will require. If you don't like what you hear, talk to someone else. There are a lot of divorce lawyers out there and rates vary a lot. You don't need to pay top dollar to find someone who will do a good job for you. (If you need an attorney but cannot afford one, see Chapter 6, section **2.** for information on how you can get financial help.)

When you're looking for an attorney, make sure you know what you want. Some people want a lawyer every step of the way, while others want one only to represent them in front of the judge. If you find a lawyer you're comfortable with and can trust, the process will be much easier on you.

2. ARE YOU SURE YOU WANT A DIVORCE?

The fact that you are reading this book probably means that even if you're not 100 percent sure you want to end your marriage, at the very least you're thinking seriously about it. Divorce, like marriage, is something that should be entered into only after a great deal of thought. While it is possible to stop divorce proceedings after they've been started, it's far easier to put things back together beforehand if at all possible.

If you have any doubts at all that this is the course of action you want to pursue, take the time to examine your options. Think about the consequences — practical, financial, and emotional — for you, your spouse, and especially your children. If there is any chance of reconciliation, seek counseling from a qualified professional. You might also want to talk to a spiritual counselor, such as a minister or rabbi.

By the same token, if you've thought things through and are certain you want a divorce, don't let any fears you may have deter you from action. Many couples who would prefer to be divorced stay together because of financial concerns and uncertainty about the divorce process and its aftermath. Don't let such worries stop you from doing what you believe is right for you. Use this book, and the other resources available in your county, to successfully and confidently complete your divorce.

3. HOW THIS BOOK CAN HELP YOU

This book takes you through the divorce process, step by step, and shows you where to turn for additional help if you need it. It tells you what forms you'll need to complete and explains all the applicable laws. It will also help you clarify and organize the decisions that you and your spouse need to make about custody, financial, and property matters.

Whether or not you decide to use the services of an attorney, this book will be a valuable resource. It will provide you with an overview so that you will have a better sense of what's going on.

It can also help save you money. For example, after reading this book, you may decide that you can do most of the work yourself and hire a lawyer for certain parts of the process only. Even if you decide to hire a lawyer for the full process, if you know what's going on and what information is required of you, you'll be better prepared for the lawyer and require less of his or her time, which will likely mean a smaller fee. (The expression "time is money" is never more true than when talking about hourly billing rates.)

Throughout the book you will find a variety of filled-in sample forms that will help show you what to expect throughout the divorce process. Keep in mind that *these forms are samples only*. Do not expect to be able to copy them exactly and use them just as they are. Some courts will not accept anything but their own official forms. The book explains how to determine which forms you need and where to get them.

4. WHAT YOU SHOULD KNOW ABOUT REPRESENTING YOURSELF

People pay lawyers because of their knowledge and expertise in one or more areas of the law. If you decide to represent yourself, without using the services of an attorney, you will have to become your own divorce expert. This book will go a long way toward helping you do just that. Here are some commonsense tips to help you stay on track:

(a) Make sure you follow all the steps in the correct order, and be very precise when you fill out your forms. Messy or incomplete forms may not be accepted by the court.

(b) Don't let yourself be rattled by legal terms. This book explains the meaning of most of the common ones you'll need, both in the text and in the Glossary at the back of the book. If there's something you don't understand that's not explained here, go to your local library and look up the term in a law dictionary; *Black's Law Dictionary* is a good one. Keep track of terms and concepts so that you can go back and refer to them later. Once you get used to the "lingo," things will seem much less complicated. Also, if you make sure you understand each step as you do it, there's less of a chance you'll get lost later on in the process.

(c) Divorce procedures in Illinois vary greatly from county to county. One valuable but often overlooked resource is the help you can get from the employees in your county circuit court clerk's office. They know the forms and procedures inside out, and they can often help out if you get stuck on something. However, it's crucial to note that they're not lawyers and are legally prohibited from giving you any legal advice (even though many of them know the law backwards and forwards). They can help you with procedural questions only. Depending on where you live, your circuit court clerk's office may have a Web site with procedures and forms you can download. At the back of the book in the Appendix, there is a list of contact information for every circuit court clerk in Illinois.

(d) At least once during the divorce process, you and your spouse will have to appear in front of a judge. This will probably be a short meeting if everything has been worked out beforehand, but even for an uncontested divorce it's important to be prepared. Judges can get impatient if they feel their time is being wasted. Also, judges are not there to provide you with legal advice or answer questions about the law. The judge you appear before will probably urge you to contact a lawyer if he or she senses that you don't know what you're doing.

(e) Always be professional, polite, and prepared throughout the divorce process. Don't ever argue with, contradict, or interrupt a judge (or your spouse, for that matter) when he or she is talking. This may sound like a small thing, but a judge has complete control over his or her courtroom. If you get on the judge's bad side, either through poor preparation or disrespect, you could be in for a very difficult time. This advice is equally true for clerks and everyone else you deal with throughout. Things will go much more smoothly and people will be more willing to help you out if you are respectful.

With the help of this book and with proper planning you'll be ready to begin. But one last note: if at any point you realize that you're in over your head, see a lawyer before it's too late. He or she may be able to get you back on track so that you can continue on your own, or you may decide to hand over the reins. Many people handle their own divorces with no significant problems, but don't be too proud to get help if you need it. A mistake made during a divorce could haunt you for years to come.

2
WHAT YOU SHOULD KNOW BEFORE YOU BEGIN

Before you even think about filing your first form, you should take some time to become familiar with some of the issues and concepts that may affect how and if you decide to proceed.

1. LEGAL SEPARATION

Legal separation is just what it sounds like — an official, legally binding declaration that you and your spouse are no longer together as husband and wife. It can be used prior to divorce or as an alternative to it, although you remain legally married. It is rarely used in Illinois, and the paperwork is nearly as burdensome as for a divorce.

Many people view legal separation as a kind of trial run for divorce. While in some respects this is true, there are some things you should know before you decide to legally separate.

1.1 The difference between legal separation and living apart

Separation does not simply mean deciding to live apart. Like a divorce, a legal separation involves a court judgment that sets out the rights and obligations of each spouse on matters such as child custody and visitation, child support, and maintenance (spousal support). Because a lot of these issues will have to be decided if you and your spouse decide to go through with a divorce, resolving them for the purpose of separating will give you something of a head start.

On the other hand, going through a legal separation will make it harder to repair the marriage (if that's what you decide to do), because you and your spouse, in both practical and emotional terms, will have already started dismantling it. If you feel there is any chance of saving your marriage, you should probably avoid pursuing a legal separation. One of you can still move out and think things over without getting a formal separation agreement.

1.2 What legal separation can do

The law dealing with legal separation provides for "reasonable support and maintenance." As mentioned above, if you are living apart from your spouse and have children and/or a need for spousal maintenance, a separation agreement can settle matters relating to custody, visitation, and support, as well as who gets to stay in the family home.

Legal separation is warranted at other times as well. Some couples with young children decide that separation is simply a less traumatic option for the family than the finality of divorce. Also, some people whose religions prohibit divorce view legal separation as a viable alternative. A separation agreement can set out some of the terms of your separate lives and provide a means of enforcing them.

Finally, in Illinois, property acquired by a spouse after legal separation is not considered marital property (meaning property belonging to both you and your spouse), so once you're legally separated, you're no longer accumulating property that will have to be divided in the event of a divorce.

1.3 What legal separation cannot do

First and foremost, separation differs from divorce in one very important aspect: you will remain legally married and unable to marry anyone else.

Just as a legal separation is not an effective means of working things out, neither is it an outright call for divorce. For this reason, it's best not to use a separation agreement as a means of sitting on the fence. If you decide to pursue a legal separation, you should have a clear plan of action in mind so that you don't remain in a holding pattern indefinitely. Choose a time when you'll firmly commit to either working things out or filing for divorce.

Also, courts generally do not get into dividing marital property or debt until a divorce proceeding has started. You and your spouse can include provisions relating to these matters in your separation agreement, but you must both agree to do so and the provisions have to be approved by the court.

1.4 Financial and practical consequences

If you do decide to pursue a legal separation, keep in mind that some of the decisions relating to it, such as custody and support arrangements, may essentially be "locked in" when the divorce proceeds unless you can show why they should be changed. For example, if you move out of the family home during a separation, it's unlikely that you'll be able to live there after the divorce. It will also be more difficult to establish a claim for custody if you've allowed the children to live with your spouse during the separation.

Judges don't generally decide final property arrangements during separation (again, unless you and your spouse have submitted an agreement that meets with the judge's approval), but as a rule they tend to avoid radical changes. They like to keep things as they are. So if, after your divorce, the continued possession of your house or another asset is very important to you, be careful not to relinquish your rights while you're separated.

1.5 The separation process

In order to obtain a legal separation in Illinois, you and your spouse must be physically living apart (some courts have found separate bedrooms to be sufficient). Also, the spouse who does the filing must be "without fault" in causing the separation. Being "without fault" doesn't mean that you have to prove flawless marital behavior; it simply means that you have not moved out, committed adultery, or in any other way seriously compromised the marriage. Generally, the spouse who hasn't moved out is the one who files for separation.

If you decide to apply for a legal separation, you must file a *petition* — the official document asking the court for a separation — in the county where the *non-filing* spouse lives, or in the county where you both last lived together as a married couple. The separation process has no bearing on the divorce filing process, and either spouse may file for divorce after a separation, regardless of who sought the separation.

Obtaining a legal separation is very similar to obtaining a divorce in terms of the filing process and the necessity of working out detailed agreements with your spouse regarding property division, spousal maintenance, and child-related issues. Read the following chapters carefully to get a general feel for the steps. If you're seriously considering a divorce at some point down the line, make sure you have a good reason for going through the hassle of a legal separation.

2. ANNULMENT

To annul a marriage means to declare it invalid. Annulments are granted in very limited circumstances in Illinois, and there are strict time limits on doing so. (**Note:** Getting a *legal* annulment is totally separate from getting a *religious* annulment. Consult with your minister or priest if you're seeking an annulment for religious reasons.)

If you and your spouse were of legal age when you married and freely consented to the marriage, and if the marriage has been consummated, you are not eligible for an annulment. You may qualify if you married a close relative or someone who was already married to someone else.

You should see a lawyer if you believe you are eligible for an annulment and you would like to pursue one. Keep in mind that even with an annulment you still have to deal with some of the same issues that accompany divorce, such as property division and issues regarding your children.

3. PREMARITAL AGREEMENTS

A premarital or prenuptial agreement (informally known as a "pre-nup") is an agreement signed before marriage that limits the rights of one or both parties property. To be valid, a premarital agreement must be in writing and signed knowingly and voluntarily by both parties. Once signed, the agreement can be changed or revoked only by another written and signed agreement.

If a premarital agreement is fair and valid at the time it's signed, it's generally difficult to get around it in the event of divorce (which, of course, is the reason premarital agreements are signed in the first place). However, if the agreement modifies or eliminates spousal support in a way that causes one spouse extreme hardship that could not reasonably have been anticipated at the time the agreement was signed, a court can, in certain cases, order the other spouse to provide support to the extent necessary to avoid such hardship.

Also, premarital agreements absolutely cannot limit a child's right to support. Provisions that attempt to do so are invalid. If you and your spouse have children, and there's a premarital provision limiting their support that your spouse refuses to change, see a lawyer.

4. MARITAL PROPERTY

Illinois law assumes that all property acquired by you and your spouse after the marriage is *marital property,* which means that the property is jointly owned. This is true regardless of whether the property is held in the name of one or both of you. For example, if you bought a car after your marriage, and registered it in your name only, it would be considered marital property.

The following types of property are exceptions to this rule and are known as *non-marital property:*

(a) Property given to one of you as a gift, a legacy (bequeathed in someone's will), or by descent (inherited property)

(b) Property acquired in exchange for property acquired before your marriage, or in exchange for property acquired by gift, legacy, or descent

(c) Property acquired after a judgment of legal separation

(d) Property you and your spouse have excluded in a valid written agreement (such as a prenuptial agreement; see section 3. above).

(e) Anything a court has awarded to one spouse from the other spouse

(f) Property acquired before the marriage (but this becomes marital property if you've transferred it into some form of co-ownership after the marriage)

(g) The increase in value of any of the above, regardless of how the increase came about

(h) Income from property acquired in any of the above ways if the income is not attributable to one spouse's personal effort

The line between "yours" and "mine" can often be blurry. When marital and non-marital property are mixed together, or *commingled,* to the point that things can no longer be separated out, it's all counted as marital property. Also, Illinois is not a community property state, but if you and your spouse own any property in a community property state (i.e., Arizona, California, Idaho, Louisiana, Nevada, New Mexico, Texas, Washington State, or Wisconsin), that property is considered marital property by the Illinois courts.

Pensions and retirement benefits are considered marital property, regardless of which spouse accrued them. However, there are special rules concerning the division of these, and you and your spouse may want to consult with an attorney or accountant to make sure they're divided fairly.

If bankruptcy appears to be on the horizon for either you or your spouse, you should file jointly for bankruptcy *before* filing for divorce. You don't want your spouse to stick you with 100 percent of the marital debts. Even though marital debts are supposed to be divided equally, if your spouse bails out on his or her portion of the agreed-upon debts, creditors can still come after you. Filing for bankruptcy will officially release you and your spouse from many of your debts and lessen your payment obligations for others. If you file for bankruptcy after divorce, keep in mind that maintenance and child support obligations are not erased by a bankruptcy filing.

Stock options you or your spouse have acquired since you got married are also considered marital property, regardless of their value and whether they're vested or non-vested. If you and your spouse cannot come to agreement, the court will decide the stock options in a way it considers fair based on a variety of factors.

4.1 Dividing the property

The division of property can be one of the most contentious and difficult aspects of getting divorced. If you and your spouse do not come to some kind of agreement on how to divide up your marital property, the court will do it for you, taking the following factors into account:

(a) The contribution of each spouse to the acquisition, preservation, or increase in value of the property, including the contribution of a spouse as a homemaker

(b) The use of the item by each spouse

(c) The value of the item to each spouse

(d) The length of the marriage

(e) The relevant financial circumstances of each spouse when the division of property is to become effective, including the desirability of awarding the family home, or the right to live there, to the spouse having custody of the children

(f) Any rights and obligations arising from a prior marriage of either spouse

(g) Any prenuptial agreement

(h) The age, health, occupation, and other money-related factors concerning each spouse

(i) Child custody provisions

(j) Whether the property is instead of or in addition to maintenance

(k) The tax consequences of property division on each spouse

Note that fault is not a factor in how courts make property allocation decisions, but the best interests of the children are taken into account. For example, the family home is generally awarded to the parent who has custody of the kids.

Because the factors listed above are so general, they don't take into account the particular needs and desires of you and your spouse regarding your property. For this reason, it's much better for the two of you to figure out on your own how to divide things if at all possible.

In order to do this, you have to account for everything you jointly own and owe. Don't worry too much about the small stuff, like a decades-old microwave oven. Focus on the big things first and work your way down. Property division details should be included in your Marital Settlement Agreement, which is shown as Sample 13 in Chapter 5.

4.2 A warning

Don't even think of engaging in any evasive or retaliatory maneuvers, such as selling off marital property or transferring it to someone else with hopes of retrieving it after the divorce. Once a divorce action is pending in court, you and your spouse are legally prohibited from transferring, selling, damaging or destroying any property, except in the usual course of business or for "the necessities of life."

If you believe you have a pressing, legitimate reason to sell or transfer something that might even potentially be considered marital property, consult an attorney. At the very least, obtain your spouse's express written permission to dispose of the asset.

5. CHILD CUSTODY

5.1 Types of custody

There are two types of child custody: physical and legal:

(a) *Physical custody* refers to where the children live — where "home" is for them. Usually one parent will have physical custody while the other has visitation rights. Alternatively, in joint physical custody arrangements, the children split their time between the two households.

(b) *Legal custody* refers to a parent's right to make important decisions concerning the children, such as schooling, medical care, and religious upbringing. Most likely, you and your spouse will share legal custody. Courts are reluctant to deprive a parent of legal custody unless serious circumstances warrant it. If you and your spouse want to share equally in key decisions concerning your child, make sure your Marital Settlement Agreement or Joint Parenting Agreement (see section **5.3**) explicitly provides for this.

5.2 Best interest of the child

The main thing courts look at when making custody determinations is the best interest of the child. In determining best interest, the judge considers all relevant issues, including the following:

(a) The wishes of the parents

(b) The wishes of the child (This takes on more importance the older the child is.)

(c) The interaction and relationship of the child with parents, siblings, and any other person who might significantly affect the child's best interest (Courts usually like to keep siblings together.)

(d) The child's adjustment to his or her home, school, and community

(e) The mental and physical health of all involved individuals

(f) Physical violence or the threat of it, or ongoing abuse, by either parent, whether directed against the child or another person

(g) The willingness and ability of each parent to facilitate and encourage a close and continuing relationship between the child and the other parent

In making custody decisions, judges do not consider the conduct of either parent, such as marital fault, unless it is relevant to the parent's relationship with the child. Unless there is abuse or some other crucial issue, it's generally believed that the maximum involvement and cooperation of both parents regarding the physical, mental, moral, and emotional well-being of their child is what's in the child's best interest.

If at all possible, you and your spouse should decide custody and visitation issues rather than letting a judge, who is probably a stranger to you and your family, decide them for you. Keep the above factors in mind when you work things out, as a judge will not approve an arrangement that's not in the child's best interest, even if you and your spouse have worked it out together.

5.3 Joint custody

In Illinois, there is no particular bias for or against joint custody. A judge will approve a joint custody arrangement only if he or she is convinced that you and your spouse will be able to make it work and have hammered out all the relevant issues.

Joint physical custody is not for everyone. It requires an extraordinary deal of cooperation and organization between you and your spouse. It can also be hard on your children, depending on how often and how far they are shuttled back and forth. If you and your spouse decide on a joint custody arrangement, you will have to include a Joint Parenting Agreement as part of your Marital Settlement Agreement (see Sample 14 in Chapter 5).

The Joint Parenting Agreement must specifically spell out each parent's rights, powers, and responsibilities pertaining to the care of the child, and for major decisions like education, health care, and religious training.

The agreement also must specify a procedure for resolving or mediating changes, disputes, and breaches of the agreement and provide for a periodic review of its terms. If you and your spouse cannot come up with a Joint Parenting Agreement that meets all these requirements, the court will come up with its own order resolving these issues, or award sole physical custody.

The court may enter an order of joint custody if it determines that would be in the best interests of the child, taking into account the following:

(a) The ability of you and your spouse to cooperate effectively and consistently in matters that directly affect the joint parenting of the child

(b) The residential circumstances of each parent

(c) All other factors that may be relevant to the child's best interest

Joint custody does not necessarily mean 50/50 parenting time. In fact, even with a joint custody arrangement, your child will still probably spend more time with one parent than the other. You and your spouse need to work out a fair arrangement regarding your child's residences, and clearly detail it in the Joint Parenting Agreement.

5.4 Visitation

If joint custody is not awarded, the parent not granted custody is entitled to visitation rights, unless the court finds, after a hearing, that visitation would endanger the child physically, mentally, morally, or emotionally. Additionally, other important people in the child's life (e.g., grandparents) can petition the court for visitation rights if they are concerned the child will be kept from them.

Your Marital Settlement Agreement or Joint Parenting Agreement must specify the details of when each of you will spend time with the child. Be as specific as possible. Don't forget to consider holidays, birthdays, school breaks and events, summer vacations, transportation issues back and forth, and family emergencies.

5.5 Modifications to the custody arrangement

Custody decisions should be viewed as permanent. They generally cannot be modified for at least two years after they're made unless there is some potential for danger to the child. And they can't be modified at all unless the court finds that there is some change in circumstances or facts not known at the time of the judgment that warrant a modification for the best interest of the child.

6. CHILD SUPPORT

Parents, whether married or not, are legally required to provide for their children's physical, mental, and emotional health. Child support payments are calculated without regard to marital misconduct, so any fault on the part of your spouse is irrelevant.

In Illinois, the minimum amount of support is determined by the following guidelines:

Number of children	Percent of supporting parent's net income
1	20%
2	25%
3	32%
4	40%
5	45%
6 or more	50%

"Net income" is the total of all income from all sources, minus the following:

(a) State and federal income tax

(b) Social security (FICA payments)

(c) Mandatory retirement contributions required by law or as a condition of employment

(d) Union dues

(e) Dependent and individual health/hospitalization insurance premiums

(f) Prior child support or spousal maintenance obligations actually paid out pursuant to a court order

(g) Certain debt repayments related to income production, necessary medical expenses, and reasonable expenditures for the benefit of the child and the other parent (not including gifts)

Assuming you and your spouse can reach an agreement about child support on your own, spell out the details in your Marital Settlement Agreement. Even though the guidelines use percentages of income, you and your spouse must indicate a fixed dollar amount of support in your agreement rather than a percentage.

You must indicate in your agreement when the child support obligation ends. A parent's obligation to pay support usually ends when the child turns 18 or is otherwise self-sufficient. However, this obligation may be extended if the child is physically or mentally disabled and incapable of self-support. It may also extend to college expenses, including room, board, dues, tuition, books, living expenses, etc.

Your Marital Settlement Agreement should also address how you and your spouse will handle your children's health insurance coverage and payment of their medical expenses.

6.1 Best interest

If you and your spouse cannot come to an agreement on child support, the judge will apply the guidelines, unless he or she determines that the best interests of your child warrant a different arrangement. The following factors are considered:

(a) The financial resources and needs of the child and the custodial parent

(b) The standard of living the child would have enjoyed if the divorce hadn't happened

(c) The physical and emotional condition of the child and his or her educational needs

(d) The financial resources and needs of the non-custodial parent

If a judge decides to deviate from the guidelines, he or she must spell out what the amount would have been under the guidelines, and the reasons for the difference. While you and your spouse have a lot of latitude in determining your own child support arrangements, if you come up with a figure that's markedly lower than what's dictated by the guidelines, you should be prepared to explain your decision.

6.2 Modifications

Because the best interests of the child are paramount, courts dislike decreasing support orders. Child support obligations are not discharged in bankruptcy, and may sometimes be only temporarily modified due to unemployment or other income-reducing factors. Also, the courts can refuse to acknowledge a voluntary decrease in income as a basis for decreased support, unless there's a good reason (such as switching to a lower-paying job that has greater potential for advancement).

6.3 Payment through the courts

Once a child support order has been signed by a judge, the supporting parent may be ordered to send payments through the office of the circuit court clerk, which will then pass the money along to the other parent. This arrangement is designed to ensure that payments can be tracked and delinquent payments caught and dealt with immediately. Payment through the courts is mandatory in certain circumstances (e.g., when the supporting parent is receiving public aid). Even if payment through the courts is not mandatory in your case, you should seriously consider this arrangement if you have any reason to believe your spouse will be unreliable with payments.

Also, if the supporting parent is employed, Illinois law authorizes automatic withholding of court-ordered support from that parent's paycheck (see Sample 22 in Chapter 5). The employer deducts the money from the supporting parent's paycheck and sends it to the court clerk. The court clerk then sends the money to the other parent. This arrangement is mandatory unless you and your spouse agree in writing to do something different. Again, this law is designed to protect a child's right to support, and you should think carefully before setting up different payment provisions.

Some people worry what their employers might think about being presented with a court order to withhold wages for child support. Fear not; this is a well-established law in Illinois, and employers are very accustomed to complying with these orders. In fact, it's illegal for your employer to fire you or otherwise discriminate against you on this basis.

6.4 Nonpayment of child support

State and federal laws provide stiff penalties for parents who fail to meet their child support obligations. Failure to pay court-ordered child support is considered being in contempt of court, and the nonpaying parent may be put on probation or even given some jail time. Driving privileges may also be suspended or restricted.

If your spouse falls behind in his or her child support payments, don't take matters into your own hands. If you try to retaliate by violating other terms of your agreement (say, by restricting your spouse's visitation rights), you'll get in trouble as well. You may want to speak with an attorney if you're having trouble getting your agreed-upon child support from your spouse. You can also contact the Illinois Child Support Enforcement division toll free at 1-800-447-4278. See their Web site: <www.ilchildsupport.com>.

7. MAINTENANCE

Maintenance, or spousal support, is less common than it once was when fewer women were in the workforce. The purpose of maintenance is to allow a spouse with diminished earning capacity time to become self-sufficient. Gender is not a factor in maintenance awards, although in practical terms it is still usually the wife who receives maintenance from the husband.

7.1 Types and amount of maintenance

Courts may grant either rehabilitative (also known as temporary) or permanent maintenance to either spouse, without regard to marital fault.

(a) *Rehabilitative maintenance* is awarded for a limited period of time so that the spouse receiving it can gather the experience and/or skills to become self-supporting. He or she must make sincere efforts to become employable and to look for a job.

(b) *Permanent maintenance* is rarely awarded unless the receiving spouse is incapable of self-support for some reason. Reasons could include a mental or physical disability, or a very lengthy period of time outside the workforce.

When considering the type and amount of maintenance to be awarded, Illinois courts consider the following factors:

(a) The income and property of each party

(b) The needs of each spouse

(c) The present and future earning capacity of each spouse

(d) Any impairment of present and future earning capacity of the spouse seeking maintenance, due to that person having devoted time to domestic duties or passing up or delaying education, training, employment, or career opportunities because of the marriage

(e) The time it will take for the person seeking maintenance to acquire appropriate education, training, and employment, and whether the person is able to become self-supporting or is unable to work because he or she is caring for a child

(f) The standard of living established during the marriage

(g) The length of the marriage

(h) The age and physical and emotional condition of both parties

(i) The tax consequences of the property division on the respective economic circumstances of the parties

(j) Contributions and services by the spouse seeking maintenance to the education, training, career or career potential, or license of the other spouse

(k) Any valid agreement between the parties

(l) Any other factor the court thinks is fair and equitable

7.2 Payment of maintenance

Like child support, maintenance amounts are automatically deducted from the supporting spouse's paycheck unless both spouses agree to an alternate arrangement. (See section **6.3** above.)

7.3 A word on property versus maintenance

If you are considering asking your spouse for maintenance, you might want to think about trying to get a greater percentage of the marital property instead, especially if you don't have children and the maintenance payments would be the only continuing tie between you and your spouse after your divorce.

8. TEMPORARY RELIEF AND INJUNCTIONS

Either spouse may ask the court for temporary maintenance, temporary child support, or custody. Further, if you fear your spouse is either endangering your children or unfairly getting rid of your joint property, you can file what's known as a *temporary restraining order* or *preliminary injunction*. These documents are filed when something needs to be acted on right away.

To get this sort of immediate, temporary relief, you'll need to file an affidavit showing a basis for one of the following types of action:

(a) Restraining your spouse from transferring, encumbering, concealing, or otherwise disposing of any property, except in a usual or necessary way (If restrained, the person must notify you of any proposed extraordinary expenditures made after the order is issued.)

(b) Preventing your spouse from removing a child from the jurisdiction of the court

(c) Preventing your spouse from striking or interfering with the personal liberty of you or your child

(d) Providing other necessary temporary relief

A court will issue this sort of relief without waiting for a response from your spouse only if it finds that "irreparable injury" — serious, lasting harm — will result if the judge waits for the response time (21 days) to elapse. You may want to enlist the help of an attorney to deal with issues of this seriousness and urgency.

9. PETS

While pets are often considered members of the family, Illinois law views them as property. For this reason, formal custody and visitation orders don't apply to pets. If you and your spouse have a beloved pet that neither of you can bear to part with, you will have to work out some reasonable means of sharing time. Put the details in your Marital Settlement Agreement. If you and your spouse can't come to an agreement, the court will award the pet to just one of you, and the other spouse will have no rights regarding the pet.

10. IF YOUR SPOUSE IS IN THE MILITARY

Special federal laws apply to members of the military service, such as the Uniformed Services Former Spouses' Protection Act (USFSPA) and the Soldiers' and Sailors' Civil Relief Act (SSCRA) of 1940. If your spouse is in the military, have him or her sign and file a waiver of SSCRA rights (see Sample 1). This form must be signed in front of a notary or a judge advocate. If your spouse refuses to sign the waiver, consult with an attorney who has experience with military divorces. You would be wise to talk to an attorney if you are or your spouse is in the military, even if your divorce is uncontested.

11. TAXES AND DIVORCE

As you might expect, a divorce carries with it tax consequences for both spouses. In particular:

(a) Maintenance is generally taxed as income for the person receiving it and is deductible as an expense by the person paying it (although there are exceptions).

(b) Child support payments are neither deductible by the person paying nor taxable for the spouse receiving them.

(c) The parent with custody of the children is entitled to claim them as dependents on his or her tax return. If there is a joint custody arrangement, the parent with whom the child spends the most time in a given year gets to claim the deduction.

(d) There are no tax consequences for the property that you and your spouse transfer to each other in the course of a divorce. However, if a piece of property has appreciated in value over the course of the marriage, you may be required to pay taxes on the increase in value when you sell it.

Don't hesitate to contact the IRS, a tax attorney, or an accountant if you have any questions about how divorce will affect your taxes. Ideally, you should do this before your divorce if you have significant assets and are concerned about how the property may be divided. You can also check out a list of frequently asked tax questions and answers on the IRS Web site at <www.irs.gov /faqs/index.html>.

12. YOUR WILL

You and your spouse are legally married until the day your divorce becomes final, so if you die without a will while the divorce is pending, some or all of your estate will go to your spouse under the laws of succession of Illinois. That may not be what you want, if a divorce is pending. It is always wise to have a will drawn up to reflect your current wishes.

Also, if your spouse is listed as the beneficiary on your life insurance policy or on other documents, you should arrange to have this changed if you want the money to go to someone else.

SAMPLE 1
WAIVER OF RIGHTS UNDER SOLDIERS' AND SAILORS' CIVIL RELIEF ACT

THE CIRCUIT COURT OF THE _Cook County_ JUDICIAL CIRCUIT,
IN AND FOR _Cook_ COUNTY, ILLINOIS

In Re: The Marriage of
_____Amber Johnson_____,
              Petitioner

and

CASE NO:_____

_____Richard Johnson_____,
              Respondent

WAIVER OF RIGHTS UNDER SOLDIERS' AND SAILORS' CIVIL RELIEF ACT

Respondent, a member of the United States military service, has been fully informed of _his_ rights under 50 App. U.S.C. §501, *et seq.*, the Soldiers' and Sailors' Civil Relief Act, in connection with the above-captioned matter and hereby knowingly and voluntarily waives all rights thereunder.

_____Richard Johnson_____
Respondent

Signed and sworn to before me
_____, ___,
_____
Notary Public

Name: _Richard Johnson_
Rank: _Private_
Serial Number: _00000-000_
Unit: _426_
Address: _888 Elm St._
City, State, ZIP: _Chicago, Il 60012_
Telephone: _555-984-0000_

3
GETTING STARTED

1. GROUNDS FOR DIVORCE

Before you file your first form, you need to decide on the *grounds* — or justification — for your divorce. Unlike many other states, Illinois is not a "no-fault" divorce state. If you want a divorce in Illinois, you have to show that you have grounds either on the basis of fault or irreconcilable differences.

1.1 Fault

To claim the grounds of fault, you must be able to prove one or more of the following circumstances:

(a) *Impotence:* Your spouse was impotent at the time of marriage and continues to be impotent.

(b) *Bigamy:* Your spouse had a legal husband or wife at the time you married.

(c) *Adultery:* Your spouse has cheated on you during the marriage.

(d) *Desertion:* Your spouse willfully left you for a year or more. This can include any time during which separation or divorce proceedings were pending.

(e) *Drunkenness:* Your spouse has shown "habitual drunkenness" for two or more years.

(f) *Drug addiction:* "Gross and confirmed" habits caused by the excessive use of addictive drugs for two or more years, meaning that the drug has become a controlling or dominant purpose of your spouse's life.

(g) *Attempted murder:* Your spouse has tried to kill you with poison or "other means showing malice."

(h) *Cruelty:* Your spouse has shown extreme and repeated physical or mental cruelty.

(i) *Crimes:* Your spouse has been convicted of a felony or another "infamous" crime.

(j) *Disease:* Your spouse has infected you with a sexually transmitted disease.

1.2 Irreconcilable differences

The grounds of irreconcilable differences is the closest thing Illinois has to no-fault divorce. You can claim irreconcilable differences as grounds for either of the two following reasons:

(a) You and your spouse have lived separate and apart for at least two years, irreconcilable differences have caused the irretrievable breakdown of the marriage, and the court determines that efforts at reconciliation have failed or that future efforts would be impracticable and not in the best interest of your family.

(b) You and your spouse have lived separate and apart for at least six months prior to the entry of judgment ending your marriage and you both agree to waive the two-year requirement. (See Chapter 5, section 3.4 for more information on waiving the two-year requirement.)

1.3 Deciding what grounds to use

The fault grounds are not used very often because they can be difficult to prove. If you're alleging adultery as grounds, for example, you need to present solid evidence supporting your claim; you can't simply state that your spouse had an affair. Also, Illinois courts generally do not consider fault when making decisions about property division, spousal maintenance, and child support. Fault isn't even factored into child custody decisions unless the misconduct directly affects the parent's relationship with the child.

For these reasons, claiming one of the fault grounds rather than irreconcilable differences usually just serves to antagonize your spouse and drag out the divorce process. However, there are two possible exceptions to this rule in an uncontested divorce:

(a) *Desertion:* If your spouse has left you, with no contact whatsoever, it may be easier for you to prove desertion than irreconcilable differences. You should be prepared to explain when your spouse left, and the efforts you've taken to find him or her. Desertion is just what it sounds like: abandonment with no contact at all (or extremely minimal contact) for at least a year. If your spouse has taken off for a year or more but is back now, or is still in semi-regular contact with you, it's probably better to claim irreconcilable differences as grounds.

(b) *Mental cruelty:* If you and your spouse have not been living separate and apart for at least six months, you cannot claim irreconcilable differences as grounds. You can, however, claim mental cruelty, which has no requirement of time lived apart. Because the hearing with the judge is a "prove-up" (meaning that you will need to prove your allegations to the judge), you will have to explain the details of your spouse's cruelty, such as —

(i) routinely making major financial decisions without you;

(ii) withholding sex;

(iii) berating you in public;

(iv) alienating you; and/or

(v) causing you physical ailments stemming from the mental cruelty, such as tension headaches, ulcers, panic attacks, depression, etc.

If you can't use one of these two exceptions, you're probably better off using the grounds of irreconcilable differences. Don't be concerned about saving face or proving that you were the one wronged; your family and friends will know your side of things, regardless of what the court documents say, and they'll probably never see those anyway.

2. MEDIATION

As you prepare to negotiate the terms of your divorce with your spouse, you may find it useful to ask for help from a mediator. A mediator can work with you and your spouse to help you come to an agreement about your divorce. Unlike an arbitrator, a mediator does not impose binding decisions; he or she will simply work with you as a neutral third party. If you and your spouse are still on reasonably good terms, a mediator can help you resolve the issues that stand between you and an uncontested divorce.

There are different ways to find mediators. Some are listed in your local Yellow Pages under "Divorce Counseling" or "Mediation." You may also want to contact the Association for Conflict Resolution (202-464-9700). Their Web site allows you to search for qualified family mediators by location <www.acresolution.org>.

Although it's rare, a judge can order something called a conciliation conference if he or she feels there is a prospect of reconciliation. The court can decide this on its own, or at the request of you or your spouse. The conference takes place at the judicial district's court conciliation facilities, or somewhere similar. The conference and anything that comes up during it are not considered in any subsequent divorce proceedings, and remain off the court record unless you and your spouse agree differently in writing.

3. WHERE TO FILE YOUR DIVORCE FORMS

Illinois is divided up into 22 judicial "circuits," each of which covers one or more counties. All of the papers relating to your divorce must be filed in the county where either you or your spouse resides. While the general process of getting a divorce is the same everywhere in Illinois, each county has its own specific forms and requirements. Cook County, for example, has a cover sheet that must be used along with all divorce-related filings (see Sample 2). For this reason, it's very important to find out what is required in the county you'll be filing in.

You will file your forms at the office of your county circuit court clerk. Don't confuse this with the county clerk's office, which is a different branch of the government. In the Appendix, there's a list of contact information for each circuit court clerk in

(Rev. 5/2/01) CCDR 0601

IN THE CIRCUIT COURT OF COOK COUNTY, ILLINOIS
COUNTY DEPARTMENT - DOMESTIC RELATIONS DIVISION

IN RE:

_____ *Jane Doe* _____   NO. _____
                                    PETITIONER

                    AND

_____ *John Doe* _____   CALENDAR _____
                                    RESPONDENT

DOMESTIC RELATIONS COVER SHEET

A Domestic Relations Cover Sheet shall accompany the initial pleading in all actions filed in the Domestic Relations Division. The information contained herein is for administrative purposes only and shall not be introduced into evidence. Please check the box designating the category which best describes the action to be filed.

GENERAL PROCEEDINGS

A	0017	☐	Praecipe for Dissolution of Marriage
B	0018	☐	Praecipe for Legal Separation
C	0001	☒	Petition for Dissolution of Marriage
D	0003	☐	Petition for Legal Separation
E	0002	☐	Petition for Declaration of Invalidity of Marriage
F	0006	☐	Petition for Legal Separation or /alternative Dissolution of Marriage
G	0009	☐	Petition for Declaration of Invalidity or /alternative Dissolution of Marriage
H	0010	☐	Joint Petition for Simplified Dissolution of Marriage
I	0004	☐	Petition for Custody only
J	0011	☐	Petition for Custody (Hague Convention)
K	0005	☐	Petition for Visitation only
L	0007	☐	Petition for Order of Protection only (which may include custody/visitation issues)
M	0085	☐	Petition to Register Foreign Judgment
N		☐	Other Petition

SUPPORT ENFORCEMENT PROCEEDINGS

O	0038	☐	Administrative Declaration of Parentage
P	0034	☐	Parentage (IV-D)
Q	0033	☐	Parentage (non IV-D)
R	0035	☐	Article X (IV-D)
S	0039	☐	Article X (non IV-D)
T	0036	☐	UIFSA

This action ☒ does \   ☐ does not   involve a minor child or children
         0100   0101

_____   _____ *Jane Doe*
_____
_____   ☐ Attorney   ☒ Pro Se
                                     Attorney Code:

DOROTHY BROWN, CLERK OF THE CIRCUIT COURT OF COOK COUNTY, ILLINOIS

Illinois, as well as which judicial circuit each county falls into. (You'll need to know the circuit when you're filling out your forms.)

Some counties have their own Web sites with divorce information and forms that you can download. Even so, it's very unlikely that you'll find all the forms you need on the Web, so it's a good idea to go to the clerk's office and ask for the forms for an uncontested *pro se* divorce. *Pro se* (pronounced "pro-say") simply means that you're representing yourself without an attorney.

For some parts of the divorce process, there will be no official county form, and you'll have to submit a document of your own that must conform to the county requirements. Make sure all the forms you submit are on standard 8½ x 11 paper. The heading of each form should match that of any official forms your county might have, with the proper information filled in. The heading will probably look something like the example below (see Sample 3). You don't need to copy the heading format exactly, but use the same language and general layout as your county uses on its forms. Use your full, legal name on all forms — no nicknames. Remember that the person filing for divorce is called the *petitioner*; the other spouse is called the *respondent*.

Some of the sample forms in this book are official forms from different Illinois counties; others are models to help you write your own forms. It's always better to use a county form if one is available, so check with your county's circuit court clerk before creating anything of your own.

Because judges and county requirements differ (some being more picky than others), it's impossible to provide samples that will be accepted in all locations at all times. If you try to file something that doesn't satisfy a particular judge or clerk, make sure you understand what the problem is so you can fix it.

4. HOW TO FILE YOUR FORMS

Chapters 4 and 5 describe which forms you need to file for your particular situation. Once you've gathered the forms you need, you need to type in the required information, or print it neatly (and legibly) in blue or black pen. If you don't have an attorney, fill in the *pro se* option you'll see on some forms.

After you've filled everything out, make several copies before filing the originals. You can call your circuit court clerk's office to find out how many copies you'll need to file. You may also need copies to "serve" on your spouse (see Chapter 5, section **2.**).

Many divorce forms need to be *verified* before you bring them to the clerk for filing. This means that you must sign them under oath in front of a notary public. You can usually find a listing for "Notaries" in your local Yellow Pages. There is a fee for having documents notarized.

Filing papers with the court sounds much more intimidating than it is. Once you have the proper forms completed, take them to the clerk's office. If everything is in order, the clerk will take your papers and stamp and file them for you. That's it. You should call first to find out the fee and how it must be paid, how many copies of the forms need to be filed, and if there are any special additional forms required.

Filing fees vary by county. At the time this book was published, a Cook County divorce filing cost $271. There will also be fees for certain later filings, such as your spouse's appearance (see Chapter 5). If you cannot afford the filing fee, you may be able to get the fee waived. See Chapter 6, section **2.1** for more information about applying for a fee waiver.

SAMPLE 3
DIVORCE FORM HEADING

THE CIRCUIT COURT OF THE _____*Nineteenth*_____ JUDICIAL CIRCUIT,
IN AND FOR _____*Lake*_____ COUNTY, ILLINOIS

In Re: The Marriage of
_____*Jane Doe*_____,
                    Petitioner

and   CASE NO: _____

_____*John Doe*_____,
                    Respondent

4
SIMPLIFIED DIVORCE PROCESS

1. CAN YOU USE THE SIMPLIFIED DIVORCE PROCESS?

If you and your spouse both agree and meet certain requirements, you can get divorced through a process known as *simplified dissolution*. This is a streamlined way of getting divorced in Illinois and is by far the easiest way to go, if you qualify.

You are eligible for a simplified dissolution only if you meet *all* of the following requirements:

(a) Neither of you are dependent on the other for support, or the dependent spouse is willing to permanently forfeit his or her right to support.

(b) At least one of you has lived in Illinois for at least 90 days.

(c) Irreconcilable differences have caused the irretrievable breakdown of your marriage, you've been separated six months or more, and efforts at reconciliation have failed or future attempts at reconciliation would be impracticable and not in the best interests of the family. (You cannot claim one of the fault grounds for a simplified divorce.)

(d) You and your spouse have no children together and the wife is not currently pregnant.

(e) You've been married for eight years or less.

(f) Neither of you owns any real estate or land.

(g) You both agree to waive all rights to spousal maintenance.

(h) The total fair market value of all marital property is less than $10,000, your combined gross income is less than $35,000, and neither of you earns more than $20,000 per year.

(i) You've disclosed to each other all assets and tax returns for all the years of the marriage.

(j) You and your spouse have created a written agreement that divides all assets valued over $100 and allocates responsibility for your debts and liabilities.

2. HOW TO FILE FOR A SIMPLIFIED DIVORCE

If you qualify for a simplified dissolution, you and your spouse must fill out and file an official county form known as a Joint Petition for Simplified Dissolution of Marriage (see Sample 4). It's important to have the entire petition — which may consist of a few separate documents — completely and correctly filled out before filing.

After you've filed your petition, you'll have to appear before a judge. The process of getting assigned to a judge and hearing time varies by county. In Cook County, for example, you'll be assigned to a hearing as soon as you turn in your petition. In DuPage County, it's your responsibility to call and set up a hearing. (When you call, be sure to ask for a hearing for a simplified dissolution.)

It's critical that *both* spouses attend the hearing with the judge. At the hearing, if everything meets with the judge's approval, he or she will sign a document called a Judgment of Dissolution that makes your divorce final and official.

Because simplified dissolution is designed to be as simple and straightforward as possible, the forms are usually very clear and complete. Some counties provide a free brochure that explains the process. Contact your circuit clerk's office for more details.

SAMPLE 4
JOINT PETITION FOR SIMPLIFIED DISSOLUTION OF MARRIAGE

(Rev. 4/11/01) CCDR 0019 A

IN THE CIRCUIT COURT OF COOK COUNTY, ILLINOIS
COUNTY DEPARTMENT, DOMESTIC RELATIONS DIVISION

IN RE: THE MARRIAGE OF

Susan Smith
                                         Co-Petitioner

                    and

Samuel Smith
                                         Co-Petitioner

No. _____

JOINT PETITION
FOR SIMPLIFIED
DISSOLUTION OF MARRIAGE

THE PARTIES HAVE READ THIS PETITION, AND PURSUANT TO LAW CERTIFY THAT THE INFORMATION IN THIS PETITION IS TRUE.

THE CO-PETITIONERS STATE:

1. **THEIR MARRIAGE REGISTRATION AND MARITAL CIRCUMSTANCES ARE:**

MARRIAGE DATE	CITY	COUNTY	STATE	SEPARATION DATE
May 22, 199-	Chicago	Cook	Illinois	April 3, 200-

HUSBAND			WIFE		
Name Samuel Smith			**Name** Susan Smith		
Residence Address 123 Anystreet		**County** Cook	**Residence Address** 456 Nameway		**County** Lake
City Chicago **State** IL		**Zip Code** 60611	**City** Highland Park **State** IL		**Zip Code** 60035
Social Security Number 123-45-6789		**Birthdate** 10/18/72	**Social Security Number** 987-65-4321		**Birthdate** 1/3/74
Occupation Dentist	**Age Now**	31	**Occupation** Store Manager	**Age Now**	30
Residence in Illinois 90 Days Immediately Before Filing	**YES**	X	**Residence in Illinois 90 Days Immediately Before Filing**	**YES**	X
	NO			**NO**	
Length of Residence in Illinois	**YEARS**	15	**Length of Residence in Illinois**	**YEARS**	4

(Rev. 4/11/01) CCDR 0019 B

Case No. _____

2. THE CO-PETITIONERS FURTHER STATE:

(a) The duration of the marriage does not exceed 8 years.

(b) Irreconcilable differences have caused the irretrievable breakdown of the marriage and the parties have been separated 6 months or more. Efforts at reconciliation have failed or future attempts at reconciliation would be impracticable and not in the best interests of the family.

(c) No children were born of the relationship of the parties or adopted by the parties during the marriage, and the Wife, to her knowledge, is not pregnant by the Husband.

(d) Neither party is dependent on the other party for support or each party is willing to waive the right to support. Each party understands that prior consultation with an attorney may have helped to determine eligibility for spousal support.

(e) Each party waives any right to spousal support.

(f) Neither party has any interest in real estate.

(g) The total fair market value of all marital property, after deducting all debts owed, is less than $10,000.

(h) Husband's gross annual income from all sources is $ __18,426__. Wife's gross annual income from all sources is $ __10,500__. The total annual income of both parties is less than $35,000. Neither party has a gross annual income from all sources in excess of $20,000.

(i) Both parties have disclosed to each other all assets and their tax returns for all years of the marriage.

(j) The parties have executed a written Agreement dividing all assets in excess of $100 in value and allocating responsibility for debts and liabilities between themselves. A copy of the Agreement, signed by both parties, is filed with this petition.

WHEREFORE, THE PARTIES SEEK A DISSOLUTION OF THEIR MARRIAGE, AND ASK THAT

A. Each party's right to spousal support be forever barred and terminated.

B. The written Agreement of the parties dividing marital assets, debts and liabilities, a copy of which is filed with this petition, be incorporated into the final order and judgment of this Court granting the petition for dissolution of marriage.

C. (Optional) That the Wife be restored to her former/maiden name:

Jones
(Type or print wife's maiden OR former name)

VERIFICATION BY CERTIFICATION

Under penalties of perjury as provided by law pursuant to 735 ILCS 5/1-109, the undersigned certifies that the statements set forth in this document are true and correct except as to matters herein stated to be on information and belief.

Susan Smith _____
Co-Petitioner Signature

Samuel Smith _____
Co-Petitioner Signature

(Rev. 4/11/01) CCDR 0019 C

IN THE CIRCUIT COURT OF COOK COUNTY, ILLINOIS
COUNTY DEPARTMENT, DOMESTIC RELATIONS DIVISION

IN RE: THE MARRIAGE OF

Susan Smith
_____
                          Co-Petitioner

and

Samuel Smith
_____
                          Co-Petitioner

No. _____

AGREEMENT

JOINT PETITION FOR SIMPLIFIED
DISSOLUTION OF MARRIAGE

WITH REGARD TO THE DIVISION OF THEIR PROPERTY AND DEBTS, THE CO-PETITIONERS AGREE THAT:

The following shall be the sole property of the Husband:

living room furnishings and electronic equipment
kitchen utensils and appliances
golf clubs
$500 (½ of joint checking account)

The following shall be the sole property of the Wife:

bedroom furnishings - bed, chair, bureau
$500 (½ of joint checking account)
dining room set

The following debts shall be the sole responsibility of the Husband:

Visa card debt - $900

The following debts shall be the sole responsibility of the Wife:

N/A

Dated this _2nd_ day of _January_, 200-.

Susan Smith
_____
Co-Petitioner Signature

Samuel Smith
_____
Co-Petitioner Signature

2807   (Rev. 4/11/01) CCDR 0019 D

IN THE CIRCUIT COURT OF COOK COUNTY, ILLINOIS
COUNTY DEPARTMENT, DOMESTIC RELATIONS DIVISION

IN RE: THE MARRIAGE OF

Susan Smith
_____
Co-Petitioner

              AND

Samuel Smith
_____
Co-Petitioner

NO: _____

AFFIDAVIT IN SUPPORT OF
JOINT PETITION FOR SIMPLIFIED
DISSOLUTION OF MARRIAGE

THE CO-PETITIONERS STATE THAT:

1. ALL PROPERTY HAS BEEN DIVIDED IN ACCORDANCE WITH THE WRITTEN AGREEMENT OF THE PARTIES FILED WITH THE JOINT PETITION.

2. THEY HAVE EXECUTED ALL DOCUMENTS REQUIRED TO CARRY OUT THE TERMS OF THE AGREEMENT.

VERIFICATION BY CERTIFICATION

Under penalties of perjury as provided by law pursuant to 735 ILCS 5/1-109, the undersigned certifies that the statements set forth in this instrument are true and correct except as to matters herein stated to be on information and belief.

Susan Smith
_____
Co-Petitioner Signature

Samuel Smith
_____
Co-Petitioner Signature

DOROTHY BROWN, CLERK OF THE CIRCUIT COURT OF COOK COUNTY, ILLINOIS

8001   (Rev. 4/11/01) CCDR 0019 E

IN THE CIRCUIT COURT OF COOK COUNTY, ILLINOIS
COUNTY DEPARTMENT, DOMESTIC RELATIONS DIVISION

IN RE: THE MARRIAGE OF

Susan Smith
_____
Co-Petitioner
            AND

Samuel Smith
_____
Co-Petitioner

NO: _____

JUDGMENT FOR
JOINT SIMPLIFIED
DISSOLUTION OF MARRIAGE

This cause was heard on the parties' Joint Petition for Simplified Dissolution of Marriage, both parties appearing in person. The Court, having jurisdiction of the parties and the subject matter and after examination of the petition and the parties, FINDS the parties' marriage registration and marital circumstances are as follows:

MARRIAGE DATE	CITY	COUNTY	STATE	SEPARATION DATE
May 22, 199-	*Chicago*	*Cook*	*Illinois*	*April 3, 200-*

THE COURT FINDS:

(a)   One or both parties have met the residency requirement of Section 401 of the Illinois Marriage and Dissolution of Marriage Act.

(b)   At filing, the duration of the marriage did not exceed 8 years.

(c)   Irreconcilable differences have caused the irretrievable breakdown of the marriage and parties have been separated 6 months or more. Efforts at reconciliation have failed or future attempts at reconciliation would be impracticable and not in the best interests of the family.

(d)   No children were born of the relationship of the parties or adopted by the parties during the marriage, and the Wife, to her knowledge, is not pregnant by the Husband.

(e)   Neither party is dependent on the other party for support or each party is willing to waive the right to support. Each party understands that prior consultation with an attorney may have helped to determine eligibility for spousal support.

(f)   Each party has waived any rights to spousal support.

(g)   Neither party has any interest in real estate.

(h)   The total fair market value of all marital property, after deducting all debts owed, is less than $10,000. The total annual income of both parties is less than $35,000.

(i)   Neither party has a gross annual income from all sources in excess of $20,000.

Susan Smith   *Samuel Smith*
_____   _____
Co-Petitioner Signature   **Co-Petitioner Signature**

DOROTHY BROWN, CLERK OF THE CIRCUIT COURT OF COOK COUNTY, ILLINOIS

(Rev. 4/11/01) CCDR 0019 F

Case No. _____

(j) The parties have disclosed to each other all assets and tax returns for all years of the marriage.

(k) The Parties have executed a written Agreement dividing all assets in excess of $100 in value and allocating responsibility for debts and liabilities between themselves. A copy of the Agreement, filed with the joint petition, has been reviewed by the Court and is not unconscionable.

WHEREFORE, IT IS ORDERED:

A. A Judgment of Dissolution of Marriage is awarded to the parties and the marriage existing between them is hereby dissolved.

B. Spousal support is terminated and forever barred.

C. Each party shall earn income and own personal property in his/her own name, possession or control free and clear of any claims of the other.

D. Each party shall be solely liable for any debts he/she may personally incur and neither shall be liable for any debt or liability incurred by the other.

E. The written Agreement filed with the Joint Petition is incorporated into this Judgment and shall be enforceable by this Court upon service of proper notice and petition.

F. (Optional) The Wife is restored to her former maiden name of _____*Jones*_____

(Type or print wife's maiden OR former name)

DATE: _____*January 2*_____ , _*200-*_

ENTER:

_____
Judge   Judge's No.

APPROVED AND AGREED

_*Susan Smith*_____   _*Samuel Smith*_____
Co-Petitioner Signature   **Co-Petitioner Signature**

DOROTHY BROWN, CLERK OF THE CIRCUIT COURT OF COOK COUNTY, ILLINOIS

5
REGULAR DIVORCE PROCESS

Most people will have to file for their divorce through the regular process. If you do not qualify for the simplified process (see Chapter 4), follow the instructions in this chapter, which explain what forms need to be filed at different times and what to expect at your hearing. Remember, different counties require different forms; the samples shown in this chapter are examples only. You can find out which forms you need by contacting your circuit court clerk's office (see Appendix).

1. THE INITIAL FILING

1.1 Petition for Dissolution

The Petition for Dissolution is the initial form you need to complete. It petitions, or asks, the court to grant you a divorce. Either you or your spouse can file the petition. The spouse who files is the *Petitioner;* the other spouse is the *Respondent.* (Some counties will use the terms *Plaintiff* and *Defendant* instead.)

The Petition must contain, at minimum, the following information:

(a) Age, occupation, and residence of you and your spouse, and the length of time each of you have lived in Illinois

(b) The date of your marriage and the place at which it was registered

(c) Whether a petition for divorce is pending in any other county or state

(d) That at least one of you has lived in Illinois for at least 90 days, and that there are grounds for divorce. At this stage the Petitioner (the filing spouse) must simply name the grounds (e.g., irreconcilable differences, bigamy, etc.), not explain them in depth.

(e) The names, ages, and addresses of all of your and your spouse's living children

(f) Whether the wife is pregnant

(g) Any arrangements for support, custody, and visitation of the children and spousal maintenance

(h) The relief sought

The Petition is where you officially ask the judge for what you want (e.g., a judgment for dissolution of marriage, joint custody, maintenance, etc.). Regardless of what you file later on, a court will be reluctant to award something that isn't asked for in the Petition, so be specific and thorough.

Sample 5 shows an example of a Petition for Dissolution. Note that the Petition must be verified (notarized) before you file it. If you would like to use your maiden name or another former name after your divorce, the best place to request this is in the Petition. Otherwise, you'll have to make a separate filing later, which will mean an additional filing fee.

1.2 Certificate of Dissolution

This certificate is required by the State of Illinois for record keeping purposes (see Sample 6). You'll need to get this form from the court clerk when you're requesting your other forms. Fill out the original (copies are not acceptable) and file it along with your Petition. Some counties may ask you to bring the Certificate of Dissolution to the final hearing instead, but have it prepared so you can file it up front if necessary.

1.3 Domestic Relations Cover Sheet

In Cook County a cover sheet is required to be included with all divorce filings (see Sample 2 in Chapter 3). Check to see if your county requires a cover sheet or has any county-specific filing requirements.

1.4 Summons and Notice

If your spouse is not cooperating with the divorce process, you will need to file a Summons (see Sample 7) along with your Petition. The Summons is an official notification to your spouse that you've filed divorce papers. After you file the Summons with the court, you need to arrange to have a copy of it delivered to your spouse (see section 2.).

If, and only if, your spouse is cooperating fully with the divorce procedure, you can skip this step. In that case, your spouse must sign an Entry of Appearance, Consent, and Waiver form in response to the Petition rather than waiting for service of an official Summons (see section 4.1).

1.5 Entry of Appearance, Consent, and Waiver

If you and your spouse are in agreement about the divorce, it is not necessary to file a Summons. Instead, you can have your spouse sign an Entry of Appearance, Consent, and Waiver form that waives the necessity of formal notice and officially signals his or her agreement to the court proceedings (see Sample 8). Like the Petition, this form must be notarized before being filed.

You or your spouse must file this form with the clerk within 30 days of when you filed the Petition. Even if you and your spouse are cooperating and file all the other necessary documents at the same time you file the Petition (see below), he or she will still need to file an Entry of Appearance, Consent, and Waiver afterwards as a formality. This step cannot be skipped.

1.6 Suburban District Stipulation (Cook County only)

If you are in Cook County in a town other than Chicago, you'll be filing your forms in one of the five suburban districts. Call the Cook County circuit court clerk to find out which satellite office serves your town. If you're filing in one of these suburban districts, you'll need to file a Stipulation and Request to Hear Uncontested Cause in Suburban Municipal District as part of your initial filing (see Sample 9).

1.7 Prepare the documents for filing

Before you go to the clerk's office with your forms, you will need to make some copies. Call the clerk and find out how many copies of the forms need to be filed. You'll also generally want at least one extra copy each for yourself and for your spouse. They should all be "originals," in the sense that you sign every copy (i.e., don't photocopy your signature).

If you are filing a Summons, you will need to have a few copies for serving the documents on your spouse (see section **2.**).

Once you have the documents prepared, take them to the circuit court clerk's office for filing. After you have filed the Petition, you must have a copy of the Petition and the Summons served on your spouse (if your spouse is not cooperating) and prepare the other documents.

Note: If you and your spouse are cooperating and a Summons is not necessary, you will likely be able to file the other documents described in the rest of this chapter at the time you file the Petition. You will need to check on the procedure for your county.

1.8 Fees

When you file your Petition, you will have to pay a filing fee. Fees for filing for divorce vary by county. Call your circuit court clerk's office for details (see Appendix). You may need to get a cashier's check or money order in advance of filing your forms because courts usually do not accept personal checks.

2. SERVING NOTICE

If you have filed a Summons, you must arrange to have it officially delivered to, or "served on," your spouse. You can arrange to have this done, for a fee, by a private process service (look in the Yellow Pages under "Process Servers"). Alternatively, a local government official, usually someone at the county sheriff's office, can perform this duty.

You'll need to provide the sheriff or process server with copies of all the documents you filed in court, as well as information about where and when to find your spouse. The summons must be personally handed to your spouse or someone else in the household who's at least 13 years old. It can't be left in a mailbox or slipped under a door, so accurate information is important.

2.1 If your spouse lives outside Illinois

If your spouse is living out of state, and you believe he or she will challenge the divorce or any aspects of it, consult an attorney before you file your Petition. Conducting a divorce across state lines can get complicated; there's a chance your spouse could be outside the reach of the Illinois courts unless he or she voluntarily consents to their authority.

2.2 If you don't know where your spouse is

Clearly, it's impossible to work out a Marital Settlement Agreement with your spouse, or even serve a Summons, if you don't know where your spouse is. However, it's still possible to get a divorce. Instead of using a Summons, you can serve your spouse through publication in a local newspaper.

Before you do that, however, you should make a solid effort to locate your spouse: call mutual friends, look in directory assistance, do some Web searching, see if he or she has left a forwarding address, etc. Keep track of the steps you've taken so that you can demonstrate to a judge, if necessary, that you've made a good-faith attempt.

Once you've searched with no luck, you can file a notarized Affidavit for Service by Publication with the court (see Sample 10). This certifies that you have made a good-faith effort to find your spouse.

You also need to file a Notice by Publication (see Sample 11). This is the document you'll have published in an effort to find your spouse. The Notice by Publication will require you to fill in a date by which your spouse must respond. Pick a weekday a little over 30 days in the future. Your notice must run for the first time at least 30 days in advance of when your spouse is required to respond.

As soon as possible after you've filed your documents (because the clock is running on your 30 days), find a local newspaper that will run your notice. The paper must be published in the county you're filing your Petition. If there isn't a newspaper published in that county, you can use a paper that's published in an adjoining Illinois county, so long as it has a circulation in the county you're filing. The paper must be approved for legal announcements. Call the paper to confirm this and ask if they can give you proof of publication. Your circuit court clerk may be able to direct you to an appropriate publication. (In Cook County, the *Daily Law Bulletin* is often used.)

Send the notice to the paper, along with a cover letter telling them that they must publish the notice at least once per week for three weeks in a row. (Sample 12 shows the type of letter you might write.) Tell them what date the first notice needs to be run by (at least 30 days before your spouse is required to answer), and check the paper to make sure it runs on time. Also, check the first run for errors, and have the paper immediately correct any you find.

If your spouse fails to respond within the specified time, you can continue with your divorce procedure by filing a Certificate and Motion for Default (see Sample 17).

If you serve your spouse through publication, and he or she never shows up, you can be awarded a divorce, child custody rights, and your share of any marital property located in Illinois. However, the court cannot award you maintenance, child support, or rights to any out-of-state marital property. This is because there are limits to the court's power over a person who has never agreed to be bound by its decisions.

3. OTHER FORMS TO FILE

This section, and the next, describe the other forms you may have to file. Some of these forms may be filed along with your Petition; others may have to be filed later. Each county has different requirements for the particulars of the filing process, so you must be sure to contact the clerk's office in your county to find out the details.

3.1 Financial Affidavit

Some judges want to see Financial Affidavits (see Sample 13) so they can determine whether the arrangements you and your spouse have worked out are fair, particularly if one of you is requesting spousal maintenance or child support. It's better to file these affidavits and be safe rather than take the chance that the judge won't want to see them. You and your spouse must each file a separate Financial Affidavit, and they must be notarized beforehand.

If your spouse is cooperating with the divorce procedure, and it is allowed in your county, you may file the Financial Affidavits along with the Petition at any time before the hearing date. If you file the Financial Affidavits with the Petition, you should note this in your Petition by adding the following paragraph:

"Petitioner and Respondent have completed Financial Affidavits detailing their respective income, expenses, assets, and debts. The affidavits are attached to this Petition for Dissolution and incorporated by reference."

Sample 15 displays a Petition with this clause incorporated, along with a clause if you also attach your Marital Settlement Agreement (see section **3.2**).

If you file the Financial Affidavits at the same time you file your Petition, you must physically attach them to your Petition by stapling all of the papers together in the upper left-hand corner. Make sure you and your spouse each get a copy of the other's Financial Affidavit.

3.2 Marital Settlement Agreement

The Marital Settlement Agreement is a detailed document explaining how you and your spouse have agreed to work out property division, maintenance, child support, and child custody and visitation (see Sample 14). It is, in effect, the blueprint for your divorce, so it should be as personalized and detailed as possible.

If you and your spouse are requesting joint custody, you must file a Joint Parenting Agreement. This can be included as part of your Marital Settlement Agreement, as it is in Sample 14, but there are certain details you must be sure to include. (Refer to Chapter 2, section **5.3** for details.) If you're not seeking joint custody, you can simply include the details about child custody and visitation in the Marital Settlement Agreement.

The Marital Settlement Agreement must be notarized, and it can be filed along with your Petition or any time before the hearing date. If you and your spouse have it prepared at the time you file your Petition, file it then, along with your Financial Affidavits. If you do this, as with the Financial Affidavits, you will have to incorporate appropriate paragraphs referring to your Marital Settlement Agreement into your Petition. You can include this paragraph in the opening clauses:

> "Petitioner and Respondent have signed a verified Marital Settlement Agreement, which is attached to this Petition and incorporated by reference. In it, Petitioner and Respondent have agreed to settle all matters pertaining to property and debt division; maintenance; and child support, visitation, and custody."

You'll also need to include the following paragraph in the section where you ask the court for relief:

> "Approve, incorporate, merge into, and make part of a final Judgment of Dissolution all the terms of the parties' attached Marital Settlement Agreement, and order Petitioner and Respondent to comply with all terms and conditions of the Marital Settlement Agreement, but that the Marital Settlement Agreement survive."

Sample 15 shows a Petition with these clauses.

Staple all four documents (the Petition, the Marital Settlement Agreement, and the two Financial Affidavits) together in the top left corner before filing.

The terms of a Marital Settlement Agreement, except for the ones regarding your children, are binding on the court unless it decides that the agreement is *unconscionable* — meaning unfair to the point of unreasonableness. If this happens, the court may request you to submit a revised agreement, or may make its own orders on these matters. Generally speaking, however, a court will leave the terms of the agreement as you've negotiated them.

3.3 Waiver of the two-year waiting period

If you're claiming irreconcilable differences as the grounds for your divorce, but you and your spouse have not been separated two years, you can still proceed if you have lived separate and apart for at least six months and you both agree to waive the two-year requirement.

In this case, you and your spouse will need to jointly file an Affidavit and Waiver of Two-Year Waiting Period (see Sample 16). File this form along with your Petition, by stapling the two forms together. Your Petition should indicate how long you've been separated and that a stipulation to waive the waiting period is attached.

4. SETTING A HEARING DATE

4.1 If you have served a Summons

If you have served a Summons on your spouse, he or she has 30 days to respond. If your spouse's response disagrees with anything you have alleged in your Petition, or indicates that he or she is being represented by an attorney, it's a good idea to hire an attorney of your own. Contested divorces are beyond the scope of this book and generally require the assistance of a good divorce attorney.

If your spouse does not respond in 30 days, then you must fill out and file a Certificate and Motion for Default (see Sample 17). The court will enter what is called an Order of Default after your form is filed.

Additionally, if your spouse is *not* in the military, you need to fill out and file an Affidavit as to Military Service (see Sample 18). Call your court clerk's office to find out when it should be filed. Special procedural protections apply for service members, and the affidavit simply confirms that those rules are not applicable to your case. (Refer to Chapter 2, section **10.** if your spouse is in the military.)

After the Order of Default has been entered, you can request a hearing with the judge (see section **5.** below).

4.2 If you have not served a Summons

If your spouse is cooperating with the divorce, and a Summons was not necessary, you can request a hearing any time after your spouse has filed his or her Entry of Appearance, Consent, and Waiver.

4.3 Setting a date

The process for setting a hearing varies from county to county. You'll probably need to schedule it with your circuit court clerk's office or someone who works directly for your judge. Be clear about what kind of hearing you need (e.g., a default hearing or a final hearing for an uncontested divorce). If you're appearing without an attorney *(pro se)*, tell the scheduler this as well.

Even if you and your spouse have filed documents together, some counties may require you to mail an official notice of the hearing date to your spouse. You'll need to fill out and file a Notice of Hearing (see Sample 19) and a Proof of Service (see Sample 20) to show that you've done this. The Proof of Service should be notarized, and both documents must be filed with the court.

5. THE HEARING

5.1 What to bring to the hearing

When you go to the hearing, you and your spouse will need to bring copies of everything you've filed so far, along with the following documents completed as much as possible beforehand:

(a) Judgment for Dissolution of Marriage (see Sample 21): This is the document that officially ends your marriage. If all goes well, the judge will sign the Judgment at your hearing. (Bring a few extra copies beyond what's required by your county.)

(b) Notice to Withhold Income for Support and Uniform Order for Support (see Samples 22 and 23): If one of you is requesting child support or spousal maintenance, you'll need to complete these forms. The withholding form authorizes the employer of the person paying support to deduct the support amounts from the wages and send them to the court, which will in turn transfer the payment to the other spouse. (For more information about the withholding requirement, refer back to Chapter 2, section 6.3.) The order makes the obligation to pay support official and binding.

(c) Certificate of Dissolution (see Sample 6): If you didn't file this along with your Petition, you need to take it with you to the hearing.

Take with you multiple copies of all documents (except the Certificate of Dissolution; you'll have just the one original of that form).

You and your spouse should carefully review all of your documents before the hearing, both those you've filed and those you're bringing along. Doing so will familiarize you with their contents and allow you to catch any errors or disagreements before you get in front of the judge. It will also allow you to answer truthfully if the judge asks if you've reviewed the documents.

5.2 The hearing procedure

The hearing is sometimes called a "prove-up" because you and your spouse will need to prove your respective allegations to the judge. Even if you're claiming irreconcilable differences, you should be prepared to discuss why you feel the differences are irreconcilable and the steps you've taken to try and solve your problems. You will be asked to testify on your own behalf, under oath.

Listen carefully to what the judge has to say, and *never* interrupt when he or she is talking. Direct your comments to the judge, not to your spouse, and do not get into an argument with your spouse in front of the judge. Address the judge as "Your Honor." Stand when he or she enters and leaves the courtroom.

Many judges dislike *pro se* proceedings because people often show up unprepared and uninformed about the law. Do your best not to be one of these people! Court proceedings are a matter of public record, so try to attend a *pro se* or default hearing before your own to give you an idea what to expect. Ideally, see if you can find a hearing that your judge is presiding over.

5.3 Finalizing your divorce

At the hearing, you can verbally ask the judge to grant the dissolution *instanter*, meaning right there on the spot. If he or she agrees to do this, your divorce will be immediately final. The judge will sign the copies of your Judgment of Dissolution at the end of the hearing. In Cook County, the copies can be "signed" by having the clerk stamp the judge's signature or name in the appropriate place on your copies at the end of the hearing. Ask the judge's clerk if that is their procedure.

You should then take these copies of your Judgment back to the circuit court clerk's office and have them certified (i.e., stamped and formally acknowledged). In some courts, this is an additional required step beyond having them stamped/signed at the end of the proceeding. There will be a nominal fee for this. It's important to take the trouble to have your divorce Judgment certified because some institutions, such as banks when considering loan applications, will not accept anything but certified copies as proof of your divorce. (**Note:** It's possible to have the Judgment certified the same day the judge signs it, but you may have to wait a few hours for your file to make its way back from the judge to the circuit court clerk's office.)

Some judges dislike granting *instanter* judgments because they want a chance to review the transcript of the hearing, which is a record of everything everyone has said. During the hearing, a court employee called a stenographer will type notes into a shorthand machine, which he or she will then transcribe into a transcript. If your judge wants to review the transcript, it will be your responsibility, before the hearing is over, to get the stenographer's contact information. Tell the stenographer you'd like a copy of the transcript of your hearing as soon as the transcript is finished. You will have to pay the stenographer the going rate (this can vary), and you will probably have to go in person to the stenographer's office and pick up the transcript. As soon as you have the transcript, go back to the circuit court clerk's office and file it. Within 28 days of the hearing date, the judge will review the transcript and, barring a major unanticipated problem, will sign your Judgment of Dissolution and your divorce will be finalized. You may be mailed a copy, but you may also have to go back to the circuit court clerk's office in person and physically check your file. Once the Judgment has been signed, follow the procedures above for getting it certified.

Your divorce papers will remain on file indefinitely with the clerk's office. It's a good idea to keep one or two certified copies on hand in a fireproof safe or safety deposit box.

SAMPLE 5
PETITION FOR DISSOLUTION

IN THE CIRCUIT COURT OF THE _Cook County_ JUDICIAL CIRCUIT,
IN AND FOR ___Cook___ COUNTY, ILLINOIS

In Re: The Marriage of

_John Knightly_____,
              Petitioner

and   CASE NO: _____

_Emma Knightly_____,
              Respondent

VERIFIED PETITION FOR DISSOLUTION OF MARRIAGE

Petitioner, _John Knightly_, *pro se*, asks this court to dissolve _his_ marriage to Respondent, _Emma Knightly_. In support of this petition, Petitioner alleges the following:

1. This court has jurisdiction over the parties and this action.

2. Petitioner is _36_ years old and resides at _123 Lilac Terrace, Chicago_ in _Cook_ County. Petitioner has resided in Illinois since _April 1982_. Petitioner's occupation is _homemaker_.

3. Respondent is _30_ years old and resides at _456 Rose Lane, Chicago_ in _Cook_ County. Respondent has resided in Illinois since _April 1982_. Respondent's occupation is _chef_.

4. Petitioner and Respondent were married on _Sept. 3, 199-_. The marriage was registered in _Huron_ County, in the state of _Michigan_.

5. Petitioner and Respondent have lived separate and apart for a continuous period since ___July 200-___, which exceeds the statutory two-year requirement, and irreconcilable differences have caused the irretrievable breakdown of their marriage. Despite honest and sincere efforts, past attempts at reconciliation have failed, and future attempts at reconciliation would be impracticable and not in the best interests of the family. No other petitions for dissolution are pending in any other county or state.

6. Petitioner and Respondent have _2_ minor children born during their marriage:

    ___Amy___, born _4/3/9-_, age _10_.
    ___Andrew___, born _4/3/9-_, age _10_.

Both children reside with _Petitioner_, their _father_, at _123 Lilac Terrace_. They have lived there for at least the past six months. _Respondent_ is not now pregnant.

7.   Petitioner and Respondent have not made any arrangements for the support, custody, or visitation of their two children, nor have they arranged for spousal maintenance.

8.   It is in the children's best interest that Petitioner be given custody of the children.

9.   Petitioner and Respondent do not have any marital property that needs to be divided. Petitioner and Respondent have already divided their property, and each party will keep the property in his or her possession.

10.   Petitioner and Respondent do not have any marital debts that need to be divided. Petitioner and Respondent have already divided their debts and allocated responsibility for them.

11.   Petitioner and the two minor children lack sufficient financial resources to provide for their reasonable needs, including expenses related to the children's education, commensurate with the standard of living that the children would have enjoyed if the marriage had not been dissolved.

12.   Respondent is gainfully employed and earning a substantial income. She is, therefore, well able to provide for child support and expenses related to the education of the children.

13.   Petitioner lacks both sufficient property, including his contemplated share of the marital property to be allocated to him, and sufficient income to provide for his reasonable needs commensurate with the standard of living established during the marriage.

14.   Respondent is gainfully employed and earning substantial income. She is therefore well able to provide for maintenance to Petitioner in accordance with his needs and commensurate with the standard of living established during the marriage.

WHEREFORE, Petitioner, _John Knightly_ , asks this court to:

A.   Enter a judgment for dissolution of marriage in favor of both parties dissolving their marriage;

B.   Award Petitioner temporary and permanent custody of _Amy & Andrew_ and make such other provisions regarding parenting and visitation as it determines is appropriate;

C.   Order Respondent to pay to Petitioner fair and reasonable support for the parties' minor children, including, but not limited to, temporary support;

D.   Order Respondent to pay for the post-high school educational expenses and support for the children of the parties;

E.   Award Petitioner fair and reasonable temporary and permanent maintenance;

F.   Order that Respondent be barred from past, present, or future maintenance from Petitioner;

G.   Restore Respondent to her former maiden name of _Woodgate_ ;

H.   Grant such other relief as it deems appropriate and equitable.

John Knightly
_____
Petitioner

VERIFICATION

Petitioner, _____, being first duly sworn, states under oath that he/she has personal knowledge of the facts and statements alleged in the foregoing Petition for Dissolution of Marriage and that they are true and correct, except for those stated to be on information and belief, and those he/she believes to be true and correct.

_____
[Petitioner's name]

Subscribed and sworn to before me this ____ day of _____, ___.

_____
Notary Public

My commission expires: _____

SAMPLE 6
CERTIFICATE OF DISSOLUTION

STATE OF ILLINOIS
CERTIFICATE OF DISSOLUTION
INVALIDITY OF MARRIAGE OR LEGAL SEPARATION

ORIGINAL

TYPE OR PRINT IN PERMANENT INK

PRINTED BY THE AUTHORITY OF THE STATE OF ILLINOIS

HUSBAND

Name of County: Cook

Court File Number

State File Number

1. Husband – Name: First — Charles / Middle / Last — Brown

2a. Social Security Number: 987-65-4321

2b. Residence – City, Town, Twp., or Road District Number: 999 Peanut Way, StripTown
2c. County: Cook
2d. State: IL

3. State of Birth (If Not in U.S. Name Country): Utah

4a. Date of Birth (Mo., Day, Year): 11/29/73
4b. Age Now: 30

WIFE

5a. Wife – Name: First — Lucille / Middle / Last — Brown

5b. (MAIDEN) LAST: Smith

5c. Social Security Number: 123-45-6789

6a. Residence – City, Town, Twp., or Road District Number: 111 Dalton Rd, Toonway
6b. County: Cook
6c. State: IL

7. State of Birth (If Not in U.S. Name Country): Michigan

8a. Date of Birth (Mo., Day, Year): 10/15/73
8b. Age Now: 30

9a. Date of This Marriage (Mo., Day, Year): 12/25/199-
9b. Place of This Marriage – City: Chicago
9c. County: Cook
9d. State (If Not in U.S., Name Country): IL

10. Date Couple Last Resided in Same Household (Month, Day, Year): 5/15/200-

11a. Number of Children Born Alive of This Marriage: 0
11b. Children Under 18 in This Household (Specify): 0

12. Petitioner–Husband, Wife, Both, Other (Specify): Husband

13a. Type of Decree (Specify: Dissolution, Invalidity, or Legal Separation): Dissolution
13b. Legal Grounds for Decree: Irreconcilable Differences

14. Number of Children Under 18 Whose Physical Custody Was Awarded To
Husband _____ Wife _____
Joint (Husband/Wife) _____ Other _____
X No children

15. Legal Representative – Name and Address (Street or R.F.D., City or Town, State, Zip)
Husband – pro se
Wife – pro se

FOR COURT CLERK ONLY

16. Date of Recording Decree (Month, Day, Year)

17. Signature of Court Clerk ▲

INFORMATION FOR STATISTICAL PURPOSES ONLY

	Number of This Marriage	If Previously Married, Last Marriage Ended By			
HUSBAND	19. First, Second, etc.	20a. By Death, Dissolution, or Invalidity? ☐ No ☐ Yes	20b. Date (Month, Day, Year)
		Specify:	
WIFE	23. First, Second, etc.	24a. By Death, Dissolution, or Invalidity? ☐ No ☐ Yes	24b. Date (Month, Day, Year)
		Specify:	

	Race	Education (Specify Highest Grade Completed)		
		Elementary or Secondary (0-12)	College (1-4 or 5 +)	
HUSBAND	18. Specify (e.g. White, Black, American Indian, etc.)	21a. Elementary or Secondary (0-12)	21b. College (1-4 or 5 +)
WIFE	22. Specify (e.g. White, Black, American Indian, etc.)	25a. Elementary or Secondary (0-12)	25b. College (1-4 or 5 +)

26. Of Hispanic Origin? (Specify No or Yes – If yes, specify Cuban Mexican, Puerto Rican, etc.)
26a. ☐ No ☐ Yes Specify: **HUSBAND**
26b. ☐ No ☐ Yes Specify: **WIFE**

VR700 (REV. 1998)   ILLINOIS DEPARTMENT OF PUBLIC HEALTH - DIVISION OF VITAL RECORDS   BASED ON 1989 US STANDARD CERT.

SAMPLE 7
SUMMONS

IN THE CIRCUIT COURT OF COOK COUNTY, ILLINOIS
COUNTY DEPARTMENT, DOMESTIC RELATIONS DIVISION

IN RE: THE ☒ MARRIAGE   ❑ CUSTODY
❑ SUPPORT OF   ❑ ORDER OF PROTECTION

Wilma Smith

PETITIONER
AND

Fred Smith

RESPONDENT
(SS # If known)   _999-99-9999_

NO:

CALENDAR:

Please serve the Respondent at:

603 Rubble Road, Apt. 4C
Chicago, IL 60614

2120 - Summons - Retd. P.S.
2121 - Alias Summons - Retd. P.S.
2700 - Return of Service P.S. - Ord. of Protect.

2220 - Summons - Retd. N.S.
2221 - Alias Summons - Retd. N.S.
2702 - Return of Service N.S. - Ord. of Protect.

SUMMONS

TO THE RESPONDENT:

The Petitioner has filed a legal proceeding against you for one or more of the following:

☒ **Dissolution of Marriage**   ❑ **Legal Separation**   ❑ **Declaration of Invalidity**   ❑ **Custody**   ❑ **Child Support**

❑ **Order of Protection under the Illinois Domestic Violence Act**   ❑ **Praecipe for Summons** *❑ **Other:** _____

YOU ARE SUMMONED and required to file your WRITTEN APPEARANCE AND RESPONSE in the Office of the Clerk of the Circuit Court Located at:

☒ Richard J. Daley Center, Room 802, Chicago, IL 60602   ❑ District 2: 5600 Old Orchard Rd., Skokie, IL 60077
❑ District 3: 2121 Euclid, Rolling Meadows, IL 60008   ❑ District 4: 1500 Maybrook Dr., Maywood, IL 60153
❑ District 5: 10220 S. 76th Ave., Bridgeview, IL 60455   ❑ District 6: 16501 S. Kedzie Pkwy., Markham, IL 60426

not later than ☒ 30 days ❑ 7 days after service of this summons, not counting the day of service.

IF YOU FAIL TO FILE YOUR WRITTEN APPEARANCE WITHIN THE TIME STATED ABOVE, A DEFAULT JUDGMENT MAY BE ENTERED AGAINST YOU AND THE COURT MAY GRANT THE PETITIONER ALL OR PART OF THE RELIEF THAT SHE OR HE IS REQUESTING IN HER OR HIS PETITION.

TO THE OFFICER: This summons must be returned by the officer or other person to whom it was given for service, with endorsement thereon of service and fees, if any, immediately after service. If service cannot be made, this summons shall be returned so endorsed.

WITNESS, _____, _____

_____
Circuit Court Clerk

Date of Service: _____, _____
[To be inserted by officer on copy left with respondent or other person]

Atty. Code No.: _____

Name: _____

Atty. for Petitioner: _pro se_

Address: _892 Rock Way_

City/State/Zip: _Chicago, IL 60611_

Telephone: _555-222-2222_

SEE REVERSE SIDE

**Service by Facsimile Transmission will be accepted at: _____
(Area Code)   (Facsimile Telephone Number)

DOROTHY BROWN, CLERK OF THE CIRCUIT COURT OF COOK COUNTY, ILLINOIS

(Rev. 12/1/00) CCDR 0001 B

NOTICE PURSUANT TO ILLINOIS SUPREME COURT RULE SCR 101(e)

ON SERVICE OF THIS SUMMONS, A DISSOLUTION ACTION STAY SHALL BE IN EFFECT, RESTRAINING BOTH PARTIES, AS PROVIDED BY STATUTE

750 ILCS 5/501.1(a) of the Illinois Marriage and Dissolution of Marriage Act includes the following:

Dissolution action stay.

a) Upon service of a summons and petition or praecipe filed under the Illinois Marriage and Dissolution of Marriage Act or upon the filing of the respondent's appearance in the proceeding, whichever first occurs, a dissolution action stay shall be in effect against both parties and their agents and employees, without bond or further notice, until a final judgment is entered, the proceeding is dismissed, or until further order of the court:

(1) Restraining both parties from physically abusing, harassing, intimidating, striking or interfering with the personal liberty of the other party or the minor children of either party; and

(2) Restraining both parties from removing any minor child of either party from the State of Illinois or from concealing any such child from the other party without the consent of the other party or an order of the court.

ANY PERSON WHO FAILS TO OBEY A DISSOLUTION ACTION STAY MAY BE SUBJECT TO PUNISHMENT FOR CONTEMPT.

* * * * * * * *

*When a praecipe for summons filed without the petition, the petitioner has commenced suit for dissolution of marriage or legal separation and the respondent is required to file his or her appearance not later than 30 days from the day the summons is served and to plead to the petitioner's petition within 30 days from the day the petition is filed. {750 ILCS 5/411 (b)}

DOROTHY BROWN, CLERK OF THE CIRCUIT COURT OF COOK COUNTY, ILLINOIS

SAMPLE 8
ENTRY OF APPEARANCE, CONSENT, AND WAIVER

IN THE CIRCUIT COURT OF THE ___Seventh___ JUDICIAL CIRCUIT,
IN AND FOR ___Sangamon___ COUNTY, ILLINOIS

In Re: The Marriage of

___Josephine Jones___,
$\qquad$ Petitioner

and   CASE NO: _____

___Napoleon Jones___,
$\qquad$ Respondent

ENTRY OF APPEARANCE, CONSENT, AND WAIVER

Respondent, _Napoleon Jones_, hereby enters _his_ appearance in the above-captioned cause.

1.   Respondent is _55_ years old and resides at _23 Water Way, Elbatown_ in _Lake_ County. Respondent has resided in Illinois since _March 1972_.

2.   Respondent is not an active member of any branch of the U.S. Armed Forces.

3.   Respondent has received a copy of the Petition for Dissolution filed in this cause. Respondent has read the petition, and understands it, and admits all of the allegations contained therein.

4.   Respondent expressly and freely waives all objections to venue and the necessity for issuance, service, and return of process in this cause and submits to the personal jurisdiction of this court. Respondent has not been involved in any prior domestic relations proceedings involving Petitioner in this or any other jurisdiction.

5.   Respondent is aware that property owned by Petitioner and Respondent may be classified as marital or nonmarital property, and that marital misconduct is not a factor in the division of said property. Respondent waives any and all rights to said property, other than those awarded in accordance with the terms of the order for Judgment of Dissolution of Marriage.

6.   Respondent agrees that this proceeding is uncontested and further consents that this cause be heard on any day chosen by the court without further notice to Respondent and that judgment be entered granting the relief requested in the Petition for Dissolution of Marriage.

___Napoleon Jones___
$\qquad$ Respondent

VERIFICATION

Respondent, _____, being first duly sworn, states under oath that he/she has personal knowledge of the facts and statements alleged in the foregoing Entry of Appearance, Consent, and Waiver and that they are true and correct, except for those stated to be on information and belief, and those he/she believes to be true and correct.

_____
[Respondent's name]

Subscribed and sworn to before me this ____ day of _____, ___.

_____
Notary Public

My commission expires: _____

SAMPLE 9
STIPULATION AND REQUEST TO HEAR UNCONTESTED CAUSE IN SUBURBAN MUNICIPAL DISTRICT

Stipulation to Hear Uncontested Cause in District
3232 - District 2   3235 - District 5
3233 - District 3   3236 - District 6
3234 - District 4   (Rev. 12/7/00) CCDR 0102

IN THE CIRCUIT COURT OF COOK COUNTY, ILLINOIS
COUNTY DEPARTMENT, DOMESTIC RELATIONS DIVISION

IN RE: THE ☒ MARRIAGE   ☐ CUSTODY

☐ SUPPORT OF   _Jane Doe_   NO.

PETITIONER
                        AND
             John Doe   CALENDAR

RESPONDENT

STIPULATION AND REQUEST TO HEAR UNCONTESTED CAUSE IN SUBURBAN MUNICIPAL DISTRICT

We, the undersigned parties, **STIPULATE AND AGREE** that all matters pending between us have been settled, agreed and compromised, freely and voluntarily after full disclosure, and we hereby **REQUEST** that this cause be heard as an uncontested matter in Suburban Municipal District _____2_____. We further **STIPULATE AND AGREE** that: ☒ we have waived our right to a **CONTRIBUTION HEARING** on the issue of fees and costs, pursuant to 750 ILCS 5/503 (j) OR
☐ a **CONTRIBUTION HEARING** will occur subsequent to the prove-up and before Judgment.

Jane Doe   _10/4/0-_   _John Doe_   _10/4/0-_
Petitioner   Date   Respondent   Date

CERTIFICATION AND AGREEMENT BY COUNSEL

We, the undersigned attorneys of record, **CERTIFY** that there are no contested issues in this cause, that all required fees have been paid, that each counsel is ready to proceed in this matter by uncontested prove-up in cases of default and we **AGREE** that the cause be heard in the above designated Suburban Municipal District. In cases where a Supreme Court Rule 298 petition required a party to make payment for fees, the party obligated to make such payment certifies that the required payment has been made. We further **CERTIFY** that we are prepared to present to the judge on the date of trial the following documents:
1) a copy of the appropriate Petition and of Respondent's Appearance, and evidence that all fees have been paid;
2) a copy of the Stipulation and Request to Hear Uncontested Cause in Suburban Municipal District;
3) a proposed Judgment including any Marital Settlement Agreement and/or Joint Parenting Agreement previously executed by the parties which may be appended;
4) an immediate Order For Support and a Notice to Withhold Income For Support; and
5) a completed Application For Child Support Services with the IV-D Agency, where appropriate.

pro se   _10/4/0-_   _pro se_   _10/4/0-_
Attorney for Petitioner   Date   Attorney for Respondent   Date

Address: _123 Blackbird Lane_   Address: _456 Robin Way_
City, State, Zip: _Northbrook, IL 00000_ City, State, Zip: _Skokie, IL 11111_
Telephone: _555-000-1111_   Telephone: _555-111-0000_
Atty. Code No.: _N/A_   Atty. Code No.: _N/A_

ORDER OF ASSIGNMENT

It is hereby **ORDERED** that this cause is assigned for prove-up to Suburban Municipal District _____
                                                                                          a.m.
on _____, _____ in Room No. _____ at _____ p.m.

ENTER:

_____   _____   _____
            Judge   Judge's No.   Date

Order/Cause Assigned for Prove-Up in District   8234 - District 4
                                                     8235 - District 5
8232 - District 2   8236 - District 6
8233 - District 3

DOROTHY BROWN, CLERK OF THE CIRCUIT COURT OF COOK COUNTY, ILLINOIS

SAMPLE 10
AFFIDAVIT FOR SERVICE BY PUBLICATION

2803 Affidavit for Service by Publication
2807 Affidavit for Service by Posting

(Rev. 10/19/01) CCG 0013

IN THE CIRCUIT COURT OF COOK COUNTY, ILLINOIS

James Filing

v.

No. _____

Mona Missing

AFFIDAVIT FOR SERVICE BY (check one)
☒ PUBLICATION ☐ POSTING

Pursuant to 735 ILCS 5/2-206 -service by publication: affidavit; mailing certificate
Pursuant to 735 ILCS 5/9-107 (Constructive Service)

Petitioner, James Filing , on oath states as to

Defendant _Mona Missing_ that:

1. Defendant (check ONE of the following):

   ☐ resides outside the state;
   ☐ has gone out of the state;
   ☒ cannot be found after diligent inquiry;
   ☐ is concealed within the state;
   therefore, process cannot be served upon defendant.

2. Defendant's place of residence is (check ONE of the following):

   ☐ (Address) _____

   _____
   (City)   (State)   (Zip)

   ☒ cannot be ascertained after diligent inquiry. His/Her last known place of residence is:

   (Address) _92 Green Bay Road_
   Lake Forest   _IL_   _60047_
   (City)   (State)   (Zip)

   Affiant: _James Filing_

Subscribed and sworn to before me this _____ day of _____, _____

Atty. No.: _____

Name: _____   Notary Public: _____

Attorney for: _____

Address: _____

City/State/Zip: _____

Telephone: _____

DOROTHY BROWN, CLERK OF THE CIRCUIT COURT OF COOK COUNTY, ILLINOIS

SAMPLE 11
NOTICE OF PUBLICATION

IN THE CIRCUIT COURT OF THE _Cook County_ JUDICIAL CIRCUIT,
IN AND FOR ___Cook___ COUNTY, ILLINOIS

In Re: The Marriage of

___Sally Burns___,
  Petitioner

and

CASE NO: _____

___Harry Burns___,
  Respondent

NOTICE BY PUBLICATION

NOTICE IS GIVEN YOU, ___Harry Burns___, Respondent, that the above-captioned case has been filed against you in this court for dissolution of marriage and other relief.

Unless you file a response or otherwise file an appearance in this cause in the office of the Circuit Court Clerk of _Cook_ County, _Chicago_, Illinois, on or before _Nov. 29, 200-_, an order of judgment by default may be taken against you for the relief requested in the plaintiff's Petition for Dissolution of Marriage.

_____Cook_____ County Circuit Clerk

Petitioner's Name: _Sally Burns_

Address: _1989 Katz St._
Chicago, IL 60606

Telephone: _555-444-5555_

October 20, 200–

To Whom It May Concern:

Enclosed please find a Notice by Publication. Please run it, as required by law, once a week for three weeks.

The law requires that the first publication of the notice be no later than 30 days prior to the response deadline — in this case, November 29, 200–. This means that the notice must run for the first time no later than October 30, 200–. If this will not be possible, please let me know as soon as possible so that I can make other publication arrangements.

Thank you very much for your assistance in this matter. Please don't hesitate to get in touch if you have any questions.

Sincerely,

Sally Burns

Sally Burns
1989 Katz St.
Chicago, IL 60606
555-444-5555

SAMPLE 13
FINANCIAL AFFIDAVIT

STATE OF ILLINOIS)
) SS
COUNTY OF WILL)

IN THE CIRCUIT COURT OF THE TWELFTH JUDICIAL CIRCUIT
WILL COUNTY, ILLINOIS

IN RE: THE MARRIAGE OF

Joseph Schmo
                Plaintiff

VS.   CASE NO._____

Susan Schmo
                Defendant

INCOME/EXPENSE AFFIDAVIT

Joseph Schmo, Plaintiff , on oath, states:

1. The parties have been married __10__ years; my age is __35__ years.

2. There are __0__ children of the marriage, aged __N/A__ .

3. I (am) (am not) residing in the marital residence.

4. My customary monthly living expenses are:

Rent/Mortgage(s)	$ 1,422
House Insurance	$ N/A
Tax Escrow	$ N/A
Food (for _1_ People)	$ 200
Doctors/Dentists	$ 20
Prescriptions	$ 50
Lien Payment on Auto	$ 600
Gas, Oil, Maintenance	$ 80
Auto Insurance/Month	$ 132
Utilities:	
Gas	$ 90
Electric	$ 120
Water and Garbage	$ 65
Telephone	$ 45
Cable	$ 30
Life Insurance	$ N/A
Clothes (for _1_ People)	$ 80
Grooming (Personal)	$ 35
Children School:	
Tuition	$ N/A
Books	$ N/A
Lunch Program	$ N/A
Babysitter	$ N/A
Clubs/Entertainment	$ 150
Gifts/Donations	$ 10
Vacations	$ N/A
Children's Activities	$ N/A
Miscellaneous:	
Books	$ 40
	$

TOTAL FIXED MONTHLY EXPENSES	$ 3,169
TOTAL MINIMUM CREDIT BILL PAYMENTS	$ 160
TOTAL EXPENSES	$ 3,329

5.   **MY TOTAL GROSS INCOME** last calendar year was $ _82,486_

    MY FEDERAL TAX REFUND last calendar year was $ _400_

6.   My employer is _self (consultant)_

    I earn $ _45_ per hour and work _160_ hours per pay period; my pay period is

    (Weekly)   **(Biweekly)**   **(Semi-Monthly)**   **(Monthly)**

    NUMBER OF EXEMPTIONS I CLAIM IS: _____

Gross Income Monthly	$ _7,200_
Less:	
Federal Withholding	$ _502_
State Withholding	$ _250_
FICA	$
Union Dues	$ _N/A_
Mandatory Retirement	$ _N/A_ _420_
Mandatory Hospital Insurance	$ _N/A_
Court Ordered Support I Pay	$ _N/A_
Other:	
_____	$ _____
_____	$ _____

    TOTAL "STATUTORY" DEDUCTIONS $ _1,172_

    NET INCOME PER MONTH $ _6,028_

    OTHER INCOME FROM ALL SOURCES $ _N/A_

    TOTAL INCOME FROM ALL SOURCES $ _6,028_

    (e.g., bonus, interest, rent, etc.)

7.

ASSETS	FAIR MARKET VALUE	DEBT
A. Real Estate		
_N/A_		
B. Vehicles		
Audi A4 (2002 model)	_$18,000_	_$16,000_
C. Bank Accounts/Investments		
Bank One checking account	_$1,500_	
D. Employment Benefits (Include Past and Present Employers)		
_401K_	_$8,000_	
E. Other Assets (of any description whatsoever)		
Sculpture	_$12,000_	
bedroom furnishings	_$800_	

8. **LIABILITIES**   **BALANCE**   **PAYMENT**

1. **Mortgages**

   N/A

2. **Auto Loans**

   Chase Auto Finance   *$16,000*   *$600/month*

3. **Credit Accounts**

   Citibank Visa   *$10,000*   *$150/month minimum*

   Sears   *$ 750*   *$ 10/month minimum*

4. **Unpaid Medical Bills**

   N/A

5. **Other Loans**

   N/A

6. **Educational Loans**

   N/A

Under penalties of perjury, provided by law in section 1-109 of the Code of Civil Procedure, I certify that the information in this Affidavit is true, correct and complete.

Date: *11/8/200-*   *Joseph Schmo*

SAMPLE 14
MARITAL SETTLEMENT AGREEMENT

IN THE CIRCUIT COURT OF THE ___*Nineteenth*___ JUDICIAL CIRCUIT,
IN AND FOR ___*Lake*___ COUNTY, ILLINOIS

In Re: The Marriage of

___*Jane Doe*___,
         Petitioner

and   CASE NO: _____

___*John Doe*___,
         Respondent

MARITAL SETTLEMENT AGREEMENT

1. Petitioner and Respondent were married on *March 22, 199-* The marriage was registered in *Bexar* County, in the state of *Texas*.

2. Petitioner is *43* years old and resides at *888 Main St., Highland Park* in *Lake* County. Petitioner has resided in Illinois since *May 1964*.

2. Respondent is *44* years old and resides at *426 Central Ave., Glencoe* in *Cook* County. Respondent has resided in Illinois since *October 1979*.

3. Petitioner and Respondent have *1* minor child(ren) born during their marriage:

    ___*Jeffrey*___, born *8/7/9-*, age *12*.

4. Irreconcilable differences have led to the breakdown of the marriage. Despite their best efforts at repairing the marriage, Petitioner and Respondent believe that reconciliation is impossible. Accordingly, Petitioner and Respondent have freely and knowingly entered into the following agreement to settle all of their marital affairs, including property and debt division; child custody, visitation, and support; and maintenance. This agreement is entered into honestly and openly, and Petitioner and Respondent have disclosed to one another all information necessary for the completion of this agreement.

THEREFORE, Petitioner and Respondent agree as follows:

A. Petitioner and Respondent shall keep their own nonmarital property, personal effects, and clothing. The following shall be the sole property of Petitioner, with Respondent waiving any and all rights or interest thereof:

The house at 888 Main Street, Highland Park, and all the furnishings currently in it
Contents of the LaSalle Bank checking account (Account #1234) - approximately $8,000

B.   The following shall be the sole property of Respondent, with Petitioner waiving any and all rights or interest thereof:

2000 Honda Prelude automobile, VIN# JX3428129871
All furniture and appliances currently in Respondent's possession
Antique wooden boat

C.   The following debts shall be paid by, and be the sole responsibility of, Petitioner:

Remainder of the mortgage held by Wells Fargo bank on the house at
888 Main Street, Highland Park (Account #248612)
Visa card bill (Account #1246381)

D.   The following debts shall be paid by, and be the sole responsibility of, Respondent:

Loan held by Chase Automobile Finance on 2000 Honda Prelude automobile
Home Depot card bill (Account #4125861)

E.   Petitioner and Respondent believe that joint legal and physical custody would be in the best interests of their child, _____*Jeffrey*_____. Petitioner and Respondent agree to cooperate to the fullest extent possible to share in _____*Jeffrey*_____'s upbringing, including all decision making regarding schooling, religious upbringing, school and other activities, discipline, and nonemergency medical care. Emergency medical decisions will be made by the parent with physical custody at that time. That parent shall notify the other parent as soon as possible of the emergency and the responsive steps taken.

F.   _____*Jeffrey*_____'s primary residence and legal residence will be with _____*Petitioner*_____, his _____*mother*_____. _____*Respondent*_____ shall have physical custody every other weekend, from 6 p.m. on Friday until 6 p.m. on Sunday. _____*Respondent*_____ shall also have custody during _____*Jeffrey*_____'s summer vacations, starting at 6 p.m. on the last day of school and ending at 6 p.m. on the evening before the first day of school. During summer vacation, _____*Petitioner*_____ shall have physical custody of _____*Jeffrey*_____ every other weekend, from 6 p.m. **on** Friday until 6 p.m. on Sunday.

The holiday custody schedule shall be as follows. Custody on a holiday shall begin at 9:00 a.m. and end at 9:00 p.m. Holidays that fall on a Friday or a Monday shall include Saturday and Sunday:

	Odd-Numbered Years	Even-Numbered Years
New Year's Day	Petitioner	Respondent
Martin Luther King Day	Respondent	Petitioner
Presidents' Day	Petitioner	Respondent
Easter Sunday	Respondent	Petitioner
Memorial Day	Petitioner	Respondent
July 4th	Respondent	Petitioner
Labor Day	Petitioner	Respondent
Veterans' Day	Respondent	Petitioner
Thanksgiving Day	Petitioner	Respondent
Christmas Eve	Respondent	Petitioner
Christmas Day	Respondent	Petitioner
Petitioner's Birthday	Petitioner	Petitioner
Respondent's Birthday	Respondent	Respondent
Jeffrey's Birthday	Respondent	Petitioner
Mothers' Day	Petitioner	Petitioner
Fathers' Day	Respondent	Respondent

In the event of a conflict between the regular custody schedule and a scheduled holiday, the holiday shall take priority. Petitioner and Respondent agree not to take _____*Jeffrey*_____ out of the state of Illinois for more than one consecutive week without the express written consent of the other. Vacations with either parent that fall outside the set custody times detailed above must be negotiated by and agreed to by both Petitioner and Respondent.

This Joint Parenting Agreement shall be reviewed jointly by Petitioner and Respondent at least once per year, or more frequently if both parties so desire. If at any time Petitioner and Respondent are unable to resolve a dispute regarding any of the issues pertaining to _____*Jeffrey*_____, Petitioner and Respondent jointly agree to seek professional mediation to resolve the dispute and to be bound by the mediator's decision. Costs of mediation will be shared equally between Petitioner and Respondent.

G.   Petitioner and Respondent agree that no maintenance will be paid to either party.

H.   Respondent agrees to pay Petitioner the sum total of $600 per month for child support. The payments will be made on the first Tuesday of every month and will start on July 1, 2003. Upon the dissolution of Petitioner and Respondent's marriage, the payments will be made by direct withholding from Respondent's paycheck, as authorized by an order to withhold income for support.

If Respondent's income goes up, he agrees to inform Petitioner and proportionately increase the amount of support payments. Respondent's child support obligations are subject to review and potential modification by a court at any time.

Child support payments will continue until ___*Jeffrey*___ has reached the age of 18, died, become self-supporting, or married. In the event that ___*Jeffrey*___ decides to pursue post-secondary education, Petitioner and Respondent each agree to pay half of the expenses, including, but not limited to, expenses for tuition, books, room and board, dues, and living expenses.

I.   Respondent will be responsible for maintaining adequate medical and dental insurance coverage for ___*Jeffrey*___. Respondent will pay all insurance premiums, as well as all deductible amounts and any medical or dental costs not covered by insurance.

J.   For as long as support payments are due, Respondent will maintain a life insurance policy in the amount of *$1,000,000* or more with ___*Jeffrey*___ named as the sole beneficiary.

K.   Petitioner will claim ___*Jeffrey*___ as a dependent on her tax return. For the current year, Petitioner and Respondent will file a joint tax return. Any refund amount will be shared equally by both, and any taxes owed will be paid equally by both.

L.   We agree that, in the event of Dissolution of Marriage, Petitioner will be known by her maiden name, *Jane Smith*. ___*Jeffrey*___ will retain the name that is on his birth certificate: *Jeffrey Doe*.

M.   Petitioner and Respondent agree and desire that, in the event of a dissolution of marriage, this Marital Settlement Agreement be approved and merged and incorporated into any such decree or judgment for dissolution of marriage and that, by the terms of the judgment or decree, they both be ordered to comply with the terms of this agreement, but that this agreement survive.

N.   Petitioner and Respondent have prepared this agreement honestly and cooperatively and have each disclosed to the other the full extent of their assets, income, and finances. Petitioner and Respondent have each completed a financial affidavit, and these affidavits are attached and incorporated by reference.

O.   Petitioner and Respondent understand the terms of this agreement and believe they are fair and reasonable. They acknowledge their right to be represented by separate legal counsel. Petitioner and Respondent agree to execute and deliver any documents, and carry out any and all acts, that may be necessary or helpful to carry out the terms of this agreement.

P.   This document represents the full and entire settlement and agreement between Petitioner and Respondent regarding their marital rights and obligations. This agreement shall be interpreted and governed by the laws of the State of Illinois.

Q.   Every provision of this agreement is expressly made binding upon the heirs, assigns, executors, administrators, successors in interest, and representatives of Petitioner and Respondent.

Signed and dated this *15th* day of *May* , 20*0*.

_____*Jane Doe*_____   _____*John Doe*_____
Petitioner   Respondent

Name *Jane Doe*   Name *John Doe*
Address *888 Main St.*   Address *426 Central Ave.*
      Highland Park, IL 60035   *Glencoe, IL 60015*
Telephone No. *555-333-8084*   Telephone No. *555-681-8121*

VERIFICATION

Petitioner, _____, and Respondent, _____, being first duly sworn, stated under oath that they had personal knowledge of the facts and statements alleged in the foregoing Marital Settlement Agreement and that they are true and correct, except for those stated to be on information and belief, and those they believe to be true and correct.

Subscribed and sworn to before me this _____ day of _____, ___.

_____
      Notary Public

My commission expires: _____

PETITION FOR DISSOLUTION INCORPORATING FINANCIAL AFFIDAVITS AND MARITAL SETTLEMENT AGREEMENT

IN THE CIRCUIT COURT OF THE _Cook County_ JUDICIAL CIRCUIT,
IN AND FOR _____Cook_____ COUNTY, ILLINOIS

In Re: The Marriage of

_____John Doe_____,
Petitioner

and

CASE NO: _____

_____Jane Doe_____,
Respondent

VERIFIED PETITION FOR DISSOLUTION OF MARRIAGE

Petitioner, _____John Doe_____, *pro se*, asks this court to dissolve _his_ marriage to Respondent, _____Jane Doe_____. In support of this petition, Petitioner alleges the following:

1. This court has jurisdiction over the parties and this action.

2. Petitioner is _36_ years old and resides at _123 Divorce Road, Chicago_ in _____Cook_____ County. Petitioner has resided in Illinois since _April 1982_. Petitioner's occupation is _homemaker_.

3. Respondent is _30_ years old and resides at _321 Separate Lane, Chicago_ in _____Cook_____ County. Respondent has resided in Illinois since _April 1982_. Respondent's occupation is _Chef_.

4. Petitioner and Respondent were married on _Sept. 3, 199-_ The marriage was registered in _____Huron_____ County, in the state of _Michigan_.

5. Petitioner and Respondent have lived separate and apart for a continuous period since _July 199-_, which exceeds the statutory two-year requirement, and irreconcilable differences have caused the irretrievable breakdown of their marriage. Despite honest and sincere efforts, past attempts at reconciliation have failed, and future attempts at reconciliation would be impracticable and not in the best interests of the family. No other petitions for dissolution are pending in any other county or state.

6. Petitioner and Respondent have _2_ minor children born during their marriage:

    _____Julie_____, born _April 3, 199-_ age _10_.
    _____Jeff_____, born _April 3, 199-_ age _10_.

Both children reside with _Petitioner_, their _father_, at _123 Divorce Road_. They have lived there for at least the past six months. _Respondent_ is not now pregnant.

7.   Petitioner and Respondent have signed a verified Marital Settlement Agreement, which is attached to this petition and incorporated by reference. In it, Petitioner and Respondent have agreed to settle all matters pertaining to property and debt division; maintenance; and child support, visitation, and custody.

8.   Petitioner and Respondent have completed financial affidavits detailing their respective income, expenses, assets, and debts. The affidavits are attached to this Petition for Dissolution and incorporated by reference.

9.   Petitioner and the two minor children lack sufficient financial resources to provide for their reasonable needs, including expenses related to the children's education, commensurate with the standard of living that the children would have enjoyed if the marriage had not been dissolved.

10.   Respondent is gainfully employed and earning a substantial income. She is, therefore, well able to provide for child support and expenses related to the education of the children.

11.   Petitioner lacks both sufficient property, including his contemplated share of the marital property to be allocated to him, and sufficient income to provide for his reasonable needs commensurate with the standard of living established during the marriage.

12.   Respondent is gainfully employed and earning substantial income. She is therefore well able to provide for maintenance to Petitioner in accordance with his needs and commensurate with the standard of living established during the marriage.

WHEREFORE, Petitioner, _John Doe_, asks this court to:

A.   Enter a judgment for dissolution of marriage in favor of both parties dissolving their marriage;

B.   Approve, incorporate, merge into, and make part of a final Judgment of Dissolution all of the terms of the parties' attached Marital Settlement Agreement, and order Petitioner and Respondent to comply with all terms and conditions of the Marital Settlement Agreement, but that the Marital Settlement Agreement survive; and

C.   Grant such other relief as it deems appropriate and equitable.

_____John Doe_____
Petitioner

VERIFICATION

Petitioner, _____, being first duly sworn, states under oath that he/she has personal knowledge of the facts and statements alleged in the foregoing Petition for Dissolution of Marriage and that they are true and correct, except for those stated to be on information and belief, and those he/she believes to be true and correct.

_____
[Petitioner's name]

Subscribed and sworn to before me this ____ day of _____, ___.

_____
Notary Public

My commission expires: _____

SAMPLE 16
AFFIDAVIT OF WAIVER AND TWO-YEAR WAITING PERIOD

2800 - AFFIDAVIT FILED
3849 - WAIVER OF 2 YEAR SEPARATION   (1/23/02) CCDR 0521

IN THE CIRCUIT COURT OF COOK COUNTY, ILLINOIS
COUNTY DEPARTMENT, DOMESTIC RELATIONS DIVISION

IN RE: THE MARRIAGE OF

Henry Bogie
PETITIONER   NO.: _____

AND

Lori Bacall
RESPONDENT   CALENDAR: _____

AFFIDAVIT AND WAIVER OF TWO-YEAR WAITING PERIOD

The undersigned parties to this cause, under oath, state as follows:

1. We have been living separate and apart, within the meaning of the Illinois Marriage and Dissolution of Marriage Act, for a continuous period of more than six months prior to the date hereof, having separated on _February 15_ , _200-_ .

2. We have attempted to reconcile the differences that arose during our marriage prior to the execution of this Affidavit and Waiver, but those efforts have failed and we have found that there has been an irretrievable breakdown of our marriage, and that further attempts at reconciliation would be impracticable and not in the best interests of ourselves or our family.

3. We hereby waive the statutory two-year waiting period pursuant to the provisions of 750 ILCS 5/401 (a)(2).

Henry Bogie   _Lori Bacall_
PETITIONER   **RESPONDENT**

Dated: _April 10_ , _200-_   Dated: _April 10_ , _200-_

Atty. No.: _____
Name: _pro se_
Atty. for: _Petitioner_
Address: _999 Pleasant St._
City/State/Zip: _Skokie, IL 60091_
Telephone: _555-555-1234_

DOROTHY BROWN, CLERK OF THE CIRCUIT COURT OF COOK COUNTY, ILLINOIS

CERTIFICATE AND MOTION FOR DEFAULT

THE CIRCUIT COURT OF THE _Fifteenth_ JUDICIAL CIRCUIT,
IN AND FOR _Jo Daviess_ COUNTY, ILLINOIS

In Re: The Marriage of

_Frances Filer_____,
           Petitioner

and   CASE NO: _____

_Arnold Absent_____,
           Respondent

CERTIFICATE AND MOTION FOR DEFAULT

Petitioner, _pro se_, certifies that there is proof of service on the Respondent on _3/3/03_. At least 30 days have elapsed since service of summons was made, and Respondent has not filed a response. Therefore, Petitioner moves that Respondent be held in default and that this matter be set for hearing.

_Frances Filer_____
                              Petitioner

Name: _Frances Filer_
Address: _19 Main St._
City, State, ZIP: _Midtown, IL 61042_
Telephone: _555-694-1111_

ORDER OF DEFAULT

IT IS HEREBY ORDERED THAT the Respondent is found in default and that this cause is assigned for default hearing before Judge _____ Calendar _____ on _____, ____, at ____ m.

DATED: _____
                                Judge

ORDER   (Rev. 6/11/02) CCG 0004

IN THE CIRCUIT COURT OF COOK COUNTY, ILLINOIS

Rosa Ross

Plaintiff

No. _____

Robert Ross

Defendant

AFFIDAVIT AS TO MILITARY SERVICE

Plaintiff, Rosa Ross _____ on oath states:

With respect to defendant _____ _Robert Ross_ _____,

_____

(the defendant is) ⟨(the defendant is not)⟩ (I am unable to determine whether the defendant is)

in the military service of the United States.

This affidavit is based on these facts:

Rosa Ross

[X] Under penalties as provided by law pursuant to 735 ILCS 5/1-109 the above signed certifies that the statement set forth herein are true and correct.

Atty. No.: _____
Name: _Rosa Ross_
Atty. for: _pro se_
Address: _9 Willow Bend Drive_
City/State/Zip: _Smalltown, IL 60124_
Telephone: _555-555-1973_

DOROTHY BROWN, CLERK OF THE CIRCUIT COURT OF COOK COUNTY, ILLINOIS

IN THE CIRCUIT COURT OF THE ___Fifteenth___ JUDICIAL CIRCUIT,
IN AND FOR ___Lee___ COUNTY, ILLINOIS

In Re: The Marriage of

___Cleo Antony___,
Petitioner

and

CASE NO: _____

___Marc Antony___,
Respondent

NOTICE OF HEARING

PLEASE TAKE NOTICE that on _July 23, 200-_, at _10:00 am_ or as soon thereafter as I may be heard, I shall appear before the Honorable ___Michael A. Smith___, or any judge sitting in _his_ stead, in the courtroom usually occupied by _him_, located at ___111 Main St., Anytown, IL___, for hearing on Petition of Motion for Dissolution of Marriage and entry of Judgment of Dissolution. You may attend the hearing if you choose.

___Cleo Antony___
Petitioner

Name: _Cleo Antony_
Address: _19 Sandy Way_
Uptown IL 94102
Telephone: _555-162-1962_

SAMPLE 20
PROOF OF SERVICE

THE CIRCUIT COURT OF THE _Cook County_ JUDICIAL CIRCUIT,
IN AND FOR _____Cook_____ COUNTY, ILLINOIS

In Re: The Marriage of

_____George Jetson_____,

Petitioner

and

CASE NO: _____

_____Jane Jetson_____,

Respondent

PROOF OF SERVICE

Petitioner certifies that a copy of the foregoing _Notice of Hearing_ was served upon _Respondent Jane Jetson_, by mailing a true and correct copy to _her_ at _842 Sky Way, Chicago, IL 60614_, her last known address, via prepaid U.S. mail on _May 12, 200-_ and depositing the same in a U.S. Mailbox located in _Chicago, Illinois_ .

George Jetson

Petitioner

Signed and sworn to before me

_____, ___,

_____
Notary Public

Name: _George Jetson_
Address: _42 Star St._
City, State, ZIP: _Chicago, IL 61284_
Telephone: _555-949-8123_

IN THE CIRCUIT COURT OF THE _Nineteenth_ JUDICIAL CIRCUIT,
IN AND FOR _Lake_ COUNTY, ILLINOIS

In Re: The Marriage of

Jane Doe ,
Petitioner

and

CASE NO: _____

John Doe ,
Respondent

JUDGMENT FOR DISSOLUTION OF MARRIAGE

The court heard a final hearing on this cause on _Sept. 12, 200-_ . Petitioner, _Jane Doe_ , and Respondent, _John Doe_ , were present in person. Respondent consented to the jurisdiction of this court by filing a valid Appearance, Waiver, and Consent.

Having reviewed all the evidence and heard the testimony presented in this case, this court finds that it has jurisdiction over the parties and the subject matter of this action.

IT IS THEREFORE ORDERED, ADJUDGED, AND DECREED BY THE COURT AS FOLLOWS:

A.   The marriage of Petitioner and Respondent is hereby dissolved;

B.   All of the terms of the Marital Settlement Agreement signed by Petitioner and Respondent, dated _May 15, 200-_ which is attached and incorporated by reference, are hereby approved and incorporated, merged into, and made part of this order. The parties are ordered to comply with all terms and conditions of said Marital Settlement Agreement, but it shall survive this order;

C.   The parties' property and debts shall be divided as set forth in said Marital Settlement Agreement;

D.   Child support obligations shall be as set forth in said Marital Settlement Agreement;

E.   Custody and visitation of the parties' child shall be as set forth in said Marital Settlement Agreement;

F.   Petitioner's name shall be restored to _Jane Smith_ as set forth in said Marital Settlement Agreement;

G.   This court shall retain jurisdiction of this cause until the terms of this judgment have been fully complied with in all respects.

So ordered this _10th_ day of _September, 200-_ .

_____
Judge

SAMPLE 22
NOTICE TO WITHHOLD INCOME FOR SUPPORT

(Rev. 1/7/03) CCDR 0556 A

IN THE CIRCUIT COURT OF COOK COUNTY, ILLINOIS
COUNTY DEPARTMENT - DOMESTIC RELATIONS DIVISION

NOTICE TO WITHHOLD INCOME FOR SUPPORT

John Jones
Petitioner

And

Jane Jones
Respondent

Case No. _____

TO: PAYOR / EMPLOYER

Name / Company _Bigco, Inc._

Address _433 Industry Road_

City _Wilmette_ County _Cook_

State _IL_ Zip _61204_

Telephone (_555_) _555-0103_

Employee/Obligor's Name (Last, First, Middle) _Jones, John_

Date of Birth _4/18/66_ Social Security No. _000-00-0000_

Residential Address _123 Pleasant St._

City _Wilmette_ County _Cook_ State _IL_ Zip _61205_

Mailing Address (if different) _N/A_

Home Telephone (_555_) _555-4567_ Work Telephone (_555_) _555-3210_

Driver's License No. (Illinois) _J123-4219-4444_ Driver's License No. (other state) _N/A_

Employee Identification No. _000-000-0000_

Custodial Parent's /Obligee's Name (Last, First, Middle) _Jones, Jane_

Date of Birth _1/9/68_ Social Security No. _111-11-1111_

Residential Address _856 Linden St._

City _Skokie_ County _Cook_ State _IL_ Zip _62014_

Mailing Address (if different) _N/A_

Home Telephone (_555_) _555-2212_ Work Telephone ( ) _N/A_

Driver's License No. (Illinois) _J456-4219-4444_ Driver's License No. (other state) _N/A_

(Page 1 of 4)

DOROTHY BROWN, CLERK OF THE CIRCUIT COURT OF COOK COUNTY, ILLINOIS

(Rev. 1/7/03) CCDR 0556 B

Child(ren) covered by Order For Support:

Name(s) (Last, First, Middle)	Sex	Date of Birth	Social Security No.
Jones, Rebecca Anne	F	9/22/199-	000-12-0000

NOTICE INFORMATION: This is a Notice to Withhold Income For Support based upon the attached Order for Support, entered by the Honorable Judge __Susan Smith_____, Circuit Court of Cook County, Illinois on ___May 15_____, 200-. By law, you are required to deduct the following amounts from the above-named employee's/obligor's income until __September 22_____, _200-_ even if this Notice to Withhold Income for Support is not used by your State.

$ __400_____ per __month_____ in current support;

$ _____ per _____ in past-due support until $ _____ is paid in full;
Arrears 12 weeks or greater? ❑ yes ❑ no

$ __120_____ per __month_____ in medical support;

$ _____ per _____ in other (specify): _____

$ _____ per _____ in other (specify): _____

Total $ __520_____ per __month_____ withheld to be paid over and sent to:

STATE DISBURSEMENT UNIT; P.O. BOX 5400; CAROL STREAM, IL 60197-5400
for payment to the obligee.

You do not have to vary your pay cycle to be in compliance with the support order. If your pay cycle does not match the ordered support payment cycle, use the following to determine how much to withhold:

$ _____ per weekly pay period. $ _____ per semimonthly pay period (twice a month).

$ _____ per biweekly pay period. $ _____ per monthly pay period.

❑ If checked, you are also required to immediately enroll the child(ren) identified above in any health insurance coverage available through the employee/obligor's employment, and withhold or cause to be withheld, if applicable, any required premiums. Premiums withheld shall be made to the health insurance plan in a timely manner. You are required to mail to the obligee, within 15 days of enrollment or upon request, notice of the date of coverage, specific information regarding the dependent benefits/coverage plan, and all forms necessary to obtain reimbursement for covered health expenses, such as would be made available to a new employee. When an order for dependent coverage is in effect and the insurance coverage is terminated or changed for any reason, you must notify the obligee within 10 days of the termination or change date along with notice of conversion privileges.

REMITTANCE INFORMATION: Follow the laws and procedures of the State of the employee obligor's principal place of employment even if such laws and procedures are different from this paragraph:

You must begin withholding no later than the first pay period occurring 14 days after the date of this notice. You must send the amount withheld to the
STATE DISBURSEMENT UNIT; P.O. BOX 5400; CAROL STREAM, IL 60197-5400
within 7 business days of the pay date. You are entitled to deduct a fee of your actual cost not to exceed $5.00 per month from the income to be paid to the obligor in order to defray the cost of withholding. The total amount withheld, including your fee, cannot exceed the amount permitted under the Federal Consumer Credit Protection Act.

(Page 2 of 4)

(Rev. 1/7/03) CCDR 0556 C

When remitting payment, provide the pay date that you withheld support; state that the order for support was entered in the Circuit Court of Cook County; Case No._____; your name, address (including county), and telephone number; the obligor's name, address (including county), social security number; and driver's license number and the obligee's name, address (including county), social security number and driver's license number.

_____*Jane Jones*_____   _____*June 22*_____, 200-

Name   ☐ Attorney of Record   ☒ Obligee   Date of Notice

ADDITIONAL INFORMATION TO EMPLOYERS/PAYORS AND OBLIGORS

☐ If checked, you are required to provide a copy of this NOTICE to your employee.

TO THE PAYOR/EMPLOYER:

1. **PRIORITY:** Withholding under this NOTICE has priority over any other legal process under State Law against the same income. Federal tax levies in effect before receipt of this NOTICE have priority. If there are Federal tax levies in effect, please contact the requesting attorney or obligee listed below.
2. **COMBINING PAYMENTS:** You can combine withheld amounts from more than one employee/obligor's income in a single payment when sending payment to the State Disbursement Unit. You must, however, separately identify the portion of the single payment that is attributable to each employee/obligor and include his/her social security number and driver's license number.
3. **REPORTING THE PAY DATE/DATE OF WITHHOLDING:** You must report the pay date/date of withholding when sending the payment. The pay date/date of withholding is the date on which the employee is paid and controls the income, i.e. the date the income check or cash is given to the employee, or date on which the income is deposited directly in his/her account.
4. **EMPLOYEE/OBLIGOR WITH MULTIPLE SUPPORT WITHHOLDINGS:** If you receive more than one NOTICE against this employee/obligor and you are unable to honor them all in full because together they exceed the withholding limit of the State of the employee's principal place of employment you must allocate the withholding based on the law of the State of the employee's principal place of employment. If you are unsure of the State's allocation law, you must honor all NOTICE of current support withholding before you withhold for any arrearages, to the greatest extent possible under the withholding limit.
5. **TERMINATION NOTIFICATION:** You must promptly notify the obligee, and the Clerk of the Circuit Court when the employee/obligor is no longer working for you. Please provide the information requested and return a copy of this NOTICE to the obligee, and the Clerk of the Circuit Court.

    EMPLOYEE'S/OBLIGOR'S NAME: _____

    EMPLOYEE'S/OBLIGOR'S CASE NUMBER: _____

    EMPLOYEE'S/OBLIGOR'S LAST DATE OF EMPLOYMENT: _____

    EMPLOYEE'S LAST KNOWN HOME ADDRESS:_____

    NEW EMPLOYER'S ADDRESS: _____

6. **LIABILITY:** If you fail to withhold income as the NOTICE directs, you are liable for both the accumulated amount you should have withheld from the employee's/obligor's income and any other penalties set by State law. You may be found liable for the total amount which you fail to withhold or pay over and fines up to $100.00 per day for each day after the 7 day grace period. See Illinois Statutes 305 ILCS 5/10-16.2, 750 ILCS 5/706.1, 750 ILCS 15/4.1 or 750 ILCS 45/20, 750 ILCS 5/507.
7. **ANTI-DISCRIMINATION:** You are subject to a fine determined under State law for discharging an employee/obligor from employment, refusing to employ, or taking disciplinary action against any employee/obligor because of child support withholding.
8. **WITHHOLDING LIMITS:** You may not withhold more than the lesser of: 1) the amounts allowed by the Federal Consumer Credit Protection Act (CCPA) (15 U.S.C. sec. 1673(b)); or 2) the amounts allowed by the State of the employee's/obligor's principal place of employment. The Federal limit applies to the aggregate disposable weekly earnings (ADWE). ADWE is the net income left after making mandatory deductions, including but not limited to: State, Federal, local taxes; Social Security taxes; and Medicare taxes. The Federal CCPA limit is 50% of the ADWE for child support and alimony, which is increased by: 1) 10% if the employee does not support a second family; and/or 2) 5% if arrears are more than 12 weeks old (see appropriate box on front).

(Page 3 of 4)

(Rev. 1/7/03) CCDR 0556 D

TO THE OBLIGOR:

1. **CONTESTING WITHHOLDING:** An Obligor may contest withholding commenced by this NOTICE only by filing a petition to contest withholding with the Clerk of the Circuit Court within 20 days after service of a copy of the income withholding notice on the obligor. The grounds for the petition shall be limited. See Illinois Statutes 305 ILCS 5/10-16.2 and 750 ILCS 5/706.1.

2. **MODIFY, SUSPEND, TERMINATE OR CORRECT WITHHOLDING:** An obligor may petition the court, at any time, to modify, suspend, terminate or correct a withholding notice. See Illinois Statutes 305 ILCS 5/10-16.2 and 750 ILCS 5/706.1.

3. **CHANGE OF ADDRESS:** The obligor must notify the obligee, the public office, and the Clerk of the Circuit Court of any changes of address within 7 days.

4. **CHANGE OF EMPLOYER:** The obligor whose income is being withheld, or who has been served with a notice of delinquency, must notify the obligee, the public office and the Clerk of the Circuit Court of any new employer, within 7 days.

5. **ANTI-DISCRIMINATION:** An Obligor may not be discharged, disciplined, denied employment or otherwise penalized by a Payor because of the Payor's duty to withhold income.

6. **ADDITIONAL RIGHTS, REMEDIES AND DUTIES:** For the obligor's additional rights, remedies and duties, if the principal place of employment is Illinois, see Illinois Statutes 305 ILCS 5/10-16.2, 750 ILCS 5/706.1, 750 ILCS 15/4.1 and 750 ILCS 45/20.

Requesting Attorney: _Jane Jones, pro se_

Address: _____

City/State/Zip: _____

Phone: _____

Fax: _____

Atty. No. _____

Obligee's Signature: _Jane Jones_

Obligee's Address: _856 Linden St._

City/State/Zip: _Skakie, IL 62014_

Phone: _555-555-2212_

Fax: _N/A_

(Page 4 of 4)

DOROTHY BROWN, CLERK OF THE CIRCUIT COURT OF COOK COUNTY, ILLINOIS

SAMPLE 23
UNIFORM ORDER FOR SUPPORT

4217	-	Continuance - Allowed	4435	-	Order on Motion to Provide Medical Insurance - Allowed
4250	-	Order, Plaintiff, Defendant or Witness to Appear - Allowed	4512	-	Order Arrearage Set (amount needed) - Allowed
4253	-	Produce Exhibits or other Records or Documents or Person - Allowed	4567	-	Order For Child Support - Allowed
4284	-	Strike or Withdraw Motion or Petition - Allowed	4568	-	Order Temporary Maintenance - Allowed
4312	-	Finding of Delinquency - Allowed	4600	-	Order Support Payments Made Direct to Petitioner
4324	-	Child Support Order Above Statutory Guidelines - Allowed	4601	-	Order Support Payments Made Direct to C.C.C./S.D.U. - Allowed
4325	-	Child Support Order Below Statutory Guidelines - Allowed	4604	-	Order Support Payments Made Direct to Respondent - Allowed
4386	-	Order to Pay Fees - Allowed			

(Rev. 12/26/02) CCDR 0107 A

IN THE CIRCUIT COURT OF COOK COUNTY, ILLINOIS
COUNTY DEPARTMENT, DOMESTIC RELATIONS DIVISION

PAGE 1 OF 6

UNIFORM ORDER FOR SUPPORT
☒ **Initial Order** ☐ **Modification** ☐ **Enforcement**

Madeline Hayes

Petitioner / ☒ Obligee ☐ Obligor

vs.

David Addison

Respondent / ☐ Obligee ☒ Obligor

Docket No. _____

IV D-No. C _____

Calendar No. _____

☐ Illinois Department of Public Aid is, or has been, granted leave to intervene.

Definitions: *Obligor* - An individual who owes a duty to make support payments pursuant to an order for support
Obligee - An individual to whom a duty of support is owed or the individual's legal representative
Payor - Any payor of income to an obligor
Unallocated Support - A total amount for maintenance and child support and not a specific amount for either

THIS MATTER coming to be heard on Petiton for ☐ Rule and/ or ☐ Modification ☐ Support ☒ Judgment

The Court Finds:

The Court has jurisdiction of the parties and the subject matter and that due notice was given by _Summons_
_____ on _May 21, 200-_ .

☒ a) The net income of the Obligor is $ _200,000_ per _year_ .

☐ b) The amount of arrearage/judgment as of the date of this order is $ _____ for child support and
$ _____ for maintenance or unallocated support as follows: $ _____ to Obligee,
$ _____ to the Illinois Department of Public Aid, and/or $ _____ to the Petitioning
State of _____ .

☐ c) The amount of child support cannot be expressed exclusively as a dollar amount because all or a portion of the Obligor's net income is uncertain as to source, time of payment, or amount.

☐ d) Retroactive child support is $ _____ from _____ to _____ .

The ☒ Obligee ☐ Obligees's Attorney ☒ Obligor ☐ Obligor's Attorney ☐ Assistant State's Attorney, being present
☐ This matter being an Interstate Case, ☐ Voluntary Acknowledgment of Paternity was signed on _____ .
It is Ordered: ☐ After hearing ☒ By agreement of the parties ☐ By default that:
David Addison , Obligor, is to provide:

☒ **MAINTENANCE** (Do not complete this section if Unallocated Support is ordered.)

Payment Amount:
Current Maintenance: $ _2,000_
Arrearage Payment: $ _____

Payments Begin: _June 1, 200-_ (date)

Payment Frequency:
☐ every week ☐ every other week
☒ monthly
☐ twice each month on _____ & _____
☐ other _____ (date)

☒ **CHILD SUPPORT** OR ☐ **UNALLOCATED SUPPORT**

Payment Amount:
Current Child Support Payment or
Unallocated Support Payment: $ _4,000_
Arrearage/Retroactive Payment: $ _____
Other Payment $ _____
Payments Begin: _____ (date)
Judgment in the amount of $ _____
is entered against the Obligor on the arrears.

Payment Frequency:
☐ every week
☐ every other week
☒ monthly
☐ twice each month on _____ & _____
☐ other _____ (date)

DOROTHY BROWN, CLERK OF THE CIRCUIT COURT OF COOK COUNTY, ILLINOIS

(Rev. 12/26/02) CCDR 0107 B

PAGE 2 OF 6

❑ **PERCENTAGE AMOUNT OF CHILD SUPPORT (Complete this section only if finding (c) is checked above.)**

In addition to the specific dollar amount of support ordered above, current child support shall be paid in the amount of _____ % of Obligor's _____ payable _____.
The Obligor is further ordered to provide income records sufficient to determine and enforce the percentage amount of child support *within 7 days* of receipt of income subject to this percentage assessment, to the ❑ Obligee and ❑ Clerk of the Court.

❑ **ADDITIONAL CONDITIONS OR FINDINGS**

   ❑ Child Support payment amount deviates from the amount required by statutory minimum guidelines. The amount of support that would have been required under the guidelines is $ _____.

     Reasons for deviation: _____
     _____
     _____
     _____

   ❑ Child Support is based on the needs of the child.

The Child/ren covered by this Order is/are:

David, Jr.   Date of Birth: _1/22/0-_   Social Security No.: _000-00-0000_

_____ Date of Birth: _____ Social Security No.: _____

_____ Date of Birth: _____ Social Security No.: _____

_____ Date of Birth: _____ Social Security No.: _____

_____ Date of Birth: _____ Social Security No.: _____

_____ Date of Birth: _____ Social Security No.: _____

☒ **PAYMENT ARRANGEMENTS**

C H E C K O N L Y O N E

   ☒ *(Payments must be sent to the STATE DISBURSEMENT UNIT if this box is checked.)*

     A Notice to Withhold Income shall be issued immediately and shall be served on the employer at the address listed in this Order. Payments shall be made payable to the State Disbursement Unit and sent to the State Disbursement Unit at P. O. Box 5400, Carol Stream, IL 60197-5400. Payments must include CASE NUMBER, COUNTY of the Court issuing this Order, and Obligor's name and social security number. Any subsequent employer may be served with a Notice to Withhold Income without further order of the Court.

   ❑ The parties have entered into a written agreement providing for an alternative arrangement for the payment of support that is approved by the Court and attached to this Order, meeting all requirements of, and consistent with, applicable law. An income withholding notice is to be prepared and served only if the Obligor becomes delinquent in paying the order of support. Payments shall be made in accordance with the written agreement of the parties attached hereto. In the event the income withholding notice is served, payments shall be made to the State Disbursement Unit as set forth above.

4386 ☒ In addition to and separate from amounts ordered to be paid as maintenance or child support, the Obligor shall pay a $36 per year Separate Maintenance and Child Support Collection Fee. This sum shall be paid directly to the Clerk of the Circuit Court of Cook County, at 28 N. Clark St. Room 200, Chicago, IL 60602, and *not* to the State Disbursement Unit.

     Docket No. _____   IV D-No. _____

DOROTHY BROWN, CLERK OF THE CIRCUIT COURT OF COOK COUNTY, ILLINOIS

(Rev. 12/26/02) CCDR 0107 C

☒ **DELINQUENCY**

If the Obligor becomes delinquent in the payment of support after the entry of this Order for Support, the Obligor must pay, in addition to the current support obligation, the sum of (a) $ _____ for delinquent child support per the payment frequency ordered above for child support, and (b) $ _____ for delinquent maintenance or unallocated support per the payment frequency ordered above for maintenance or unallocated support, until the delinquency is paid in full. (This additional amount, the total of (a) and (b), shall not be less than 20 percent of the total of the current support amount and the amount to be paid for payment of any arrearage stated in the Order for Support.) A support obligation, or any portion of a support obligation which becomes due and remains unpaid for 30 days or more, shall accrue interest at the rate of 9% per annum.

☒ **TERMINATION**

This Obligation to pay child support terminates on _____ - _____ - _____ unless modified by written order of the Court. This termination date does not apply to any arrearage that may remain unpaid on that date.

☐ **MEDICAL INSURANCE**

The ☐ Obligor, ☐ Obligee, ☐ Obligor *and* Obligee, shall provide health insurance for the child(ren): ☐ as provided in previous order entered on _____; ☐ enrolling them in any health insurance coverage available through the ☐ Obligor's, ☐ Obligee's, ☐ Obligor's *and* Obligee's, employment or ☐ securing a private health insurance policy, accepted by the Obligor and Obligee or approved by the Court, which names the child(ren) as beneficiary. The Obligor shall provide to the Obligee a copy of the insurance policy and the insurance card within *45 days*. The employer or labor union or trade union shall disclose information concerning dependent coverage plans whether or not a court order for medical support has been entered. 750 ILCS 5/505.2.

☐ The Obligor is liable for _____ % of medical expenses incurred by the minor child(ren) and not covered by insurance.

4284 ☐ The issue of medical insurance is withdrawn.

It is further ordered that (except when the Court finds that the physical, mental or emotional health of a party or that of a minor child, or both, would be seriously endangered by disclosure of the party's address:)

The Obligor shall give written notice to the Clerk of the Court, and *if* a party is receiving child and spouse services under Article X of the Illinois Public Aid Code, to the Department of Public Aid, *within 7 days,* of:

- any new residential, mailing address or telephone number;
- the name, address and phone number of any new employer, and;
- the policy name and identifying number(s) of health insurance coverage available.

The Obligor shall submit a written report of termination of employment and of new employment, including name and address of the new employer, to the Clerk of the Court and the Obligee *within 10 days.* Obligor and Obligee shall advise each other of a change of residence *within 5 days* except when the Court finds that the physical, mental or emotional health of a party or that of a minor child, or both, would be seriously endangered by disclosure of the party's address. An Obligee receiving payments through income withholding shall notify the Clerk of the Court and the State Disbursement Unit *within 7 days,* of change in residence. The Obligor and Obligee shall report to the Clerk of the Court any change of information included in the Child Support Data Sheet (Exhibit 1) *within 5 business days* of such a change.

☐ **UNEMPLOYMENT:**

☐ Respondent is unemployed and is ordered to seek employment. The Respondent must report periodically to the court with a diary listing the name, address, telephone number and contact person of each employer with which he or she has sought employment.

Docket No. _____   IV D-No. _____

DOROTHY BROWN, CLERK OF THE CIRCUIT COURT OF COOK COUNTY, ILLINOIS

(Rev. 12/26/02) **CCDR 0107 D**

PAGE 4 OF 6

❏ Respondent is ordered to report to the Department of Employment Security for job search services or to complete an application with the local Job Training Partnership Act provider for participation in job search, training or work programs.

❏ Respondent is unemployed and is ordered to put forth a diligent effort to obtain employment and to cooperate with all instructions of the Illinois Department of Public Aid. The Respondent is ordered to report immediately to the Illinois Department of Public Aid's Non-Custodial Parent Services Unit, 32 W. Randolph St., 14th Floor, for assessment and assignment into the court monitored Job Search program or Earnfare program. *Upon finding employment, the Respondent shall notify IDPA in writing at 32 W. Randolph St., 9th Floor, Chicago, IL 60601 within seven days.* The Respondent must submit the name and address of the employer, the start date, and the rate of pay to the IDPA Non-Custodial Parent Services Unit. The Respondent's failure to comply with the requirements of this order may result in the State's Attorney seeking a contempt of court order. (Note: Earnfare requires a $50.00 minimum support order.)

❏ *GENETIC TEST REIMBURSEMENT:* Obligor shall pay $ _____ to the Illinois Department of Public Aid (IDPA) for a genetic test reimbursement. Payments must be made in lump sum or installments by personal check or money order payable to Illinois Department of Public Aid and either mailed to: Illinois Department of Public Aid, Title IV-D Accounting Unit, P.O. Box 19138, Springfield, IL 62705-9138, or conveyed as otherwise directed by the Court. Payment must include IV-D number as shown on this Order.

This Order does not preclude the Illinois Department of Public Aid from collecting any arrearage established by or which may accrue under this Order for Support by use of the offset provisions of Section 6402(c) of the Internal Revenue Code of 1954, and 15 ILCS 405/10.05(a) as amended. Such arreage shall be considered as "past due" or "due and payable" within the meaning of said statutory provisions. This order does not preclude the placing of a lien on real and personal assets or initiating a proceeding for garnishment, attachment of sequestration pursuant to law and the Code of Civil Procedure.

This order of support supercedes any and all prior orders of support under this case number.

❏ Other: _____
_____
_____
_____
_____
_____
_____
_____

   ❏ This cause is continued for _____ to _____ ,

at _____ M. ❏ without further notice ❏ without further notice to Petitioner

❏ without further notice to Respondent.

FAILURE TO APPEAR MAY RESULT IN ENTRY OF A DEFAULT JUDGMENT.

❏ FOR EXPEDITED CHILD SUPPORT CASES ONLY:

NOTICE OF RIGHT TO REQUEST A JUDICIAL HEARING: You have a right to request a Judicial Hearing. If either party does not agree to the recommended Order or any part thereof, this case will be transferred for an immediate Judicial Hearing.

   Docket No. _____   IV D-No. _____

DOROTHY BROWN, CLERK OF THE CIRCUIT COURT OF COOK COUNTY, ILLINOIS

This order may be vacated or amended within 30 days of its entry. This order is not valid until signed by a judge.

So recommended to this Court by the Hearing Officer this _____ day of _____, _____

_____
Hearing Officer's Signature

_____*Madeline Hayes*_____   _____*David Addison*_____
Petitioner/ Obligee's Signature   **Respondent/ Obligor's Signature**

_____*pro se*_____   _____*pro se*_____
Petitioner/ Obligee's Attorney's Signature   **Respondent/ Obligor's Attorney's Signature**

The support obligation herein required under this order, or any portion of the obligation, which becomes due and remains unpaid for 30 days or more shall accrue simple interest at the rate of 9% per anum.

FAILURE TO OBEY ANY OF THE PROVISIONS OF THIS ORDER MAY RESULT IN A FINDING OF CONTEMPT OF COURT.

_____   _____
Date   **Judge**   **Judge's No.**

Prepared by:

Atty. Code No.: _____
Name: _____*Madeline Hayes*_____
Atty. for: _____*pro se*_____
Address: _____*227 Blue Moon Way*_____
City/State/Zip: _*Lalaland, IL 00000*_____
Telephone: _*555-555-8214*_____

DOROTHY BROWN, CLERK OF THE CIRCUIT COURT OF COOK COUNTY, ILLINOIS

(Rev. 12/26/02) CCDR 0107 F

PAGE 6 OF 6

Madeline Hayes
Plaintiff/Petitioner

vs.

David Addison
Defendant/Respondent

Case No.: _____

County: _____

Date: _____

CHILD SUPPORT DATA SHEET

OBLIGOR INFORMATION	OBLIGEE INFORMATION
Last Name: *Addison*	Last Name: *Hayes*
First Name: *David* Middle In: ___	First Name: *Madeline* Middle In: ___
Complete *Residential* Address: *422 Lakeside St. Chicago, IL 12353*	Complete *Residential* Address: *227 Blue Moon Way Lalaland, IL 00000*
Complete Mailing Address (*If other than above*): *same*	Complete Mailing Address (*If other than above*): *same*
Date of Birth: *4/17/66*	Date of Birth: *9/27/68*
Driver's License No.: *A12694123*	Driver's License No.: *H30165822*
*Social Security No. *000-00-0000*	*Social Security No. *111-11-1111*
Home Phone Number: *555-888-8888*	Home Phone Number: *555-555-8214*
Employer(s) Name/Company: *Big Corp. Inc.*	Employer(s) Name/Company: *Small Corp. Inc.*
Employer(s) Address: *825 Industrial Way Citytown, IL 99999*	Employer(s) Address: *426 Commerce St. Watertown, IL 00000*
Employer(s) ID Number: *742138245*	Employer(s) ID Number: *987651234*
Work Phone Number (*555*) *555-021*	Work Phone Number (*555*) *555-9204*

CHILD/CHILDREN INFORMATION

	LAST	FIRST	MIDDLE INITIAL	DATE OF BIRTH	SOCIAL SECURITY NUMBER
1.	*Addison*	*David*		*1/22/0-*	*000-22-0000*
2.					
3.					
4.					
5.					

(If more space is needed, attach an additional sheet.)

* If Obligor is not a US citizen, so indicate and provide the Obligor's alien registration number, passport number and home country's social security or national health number.

DOROTHY BROWN, CLERK OF THE CIRCUIT COURT OF COOK COUNTY, ILLINOIS

6
SPECIAL CIRCUMSTANCES — GETTING HELP

1. IF YOU ARE BEING ABUSED

If you and/or your children are being abused by your spouse, you can ask the court for an Order of Protection (see Sample 24). However, you will probably need to take other steps as well to keep yourself and your children safe. The Illinois Coalition Against Domestic Violence is a good source for information and resources (phone 217-789-2830, or go to their Web site at <www.ilcadv.org/legal/fed_firearm_laws.htm>). Call 911 or your local police department if you or your children are in immediate danger.

Remember also that you can ask the court for a temporary restraining order if necessary. Refer back to chapter 2, section 8. for more information.

As was mentioned in the beginning of this book, it is generally a very risky idea to pursue a divorce against an abusive spouse without professional legal assistance.

2. IF YOU NEED FINANCIAL HELP

2.1 Waiver of fees

If you believe that you will be unable to pay the necessary filing fees for your divorce, you can file an Application to Sue as an Indigent (see Sample 25). File this with the clerk before you file your Petition for Dissolution. You will have to explain why you believe you should be exempt from the fees, so be prepared to present proof of your financial situation.

If the application is approved, you will be able to file your divorce Petition without paying the standard filing fee. If it's not approved, this won't be held against you in any way for the rest of the case; it just means that you'll have to pay the fees.

2.2 Legal aid

If you believe you need a lawyer to help you out with some or all of your case but you can't afford one, here are some resources that can provide you with information and assistance:

Coordinated Advice and Referral Program for Legal Services
Telephone: 312-738-9200
Web site: www.carpls.org

Illinois Technology Center's IllinoisLawHelp.org Web Page
Web site: www.illinoislawhelp.org

Land of Lincoln Legal Assistance Foundation
Telephone: 1-877-342-7891

Prairie State Legal Services
Telephone: 815-965-2134
Web site: www.pslegal.org

The Self Help Legal Center
Telephone: 618-453-3217
Web site: www.law.siu.edu/selfhelp

SAMPLE 24
ORDER OF PROTECTION*

(This form replaces CCG-82-2)   (Rev. 4/7/03) CCDR 0802 A

IN THE CIRCUIT COURT OF COOK COUNTY, ILLINOIS

People ex rel. _____

_____ on behalf of

_____ self and/or on behalf of

Case No. _____

❑ Independent Proceeding
❑ Other Civil Proceeding
    (specify) _____

_____

                                          Petitioner

                    vs.

❑ Criminal Proceeding
❑ Juvenile Proceeding

_____

                                          Respondent

FINDINGS
ORDER OF PROTECTION

❑ Emergency   ❑ Interim   ❑ Plenary

[Finding solely applicable to an ex parte Emergency Order]

The Court, having examined the Petition filed in this case, as well as the person presenting the petition, under oath, FINDS THAT:

❑ The averments presented are sufficient to grant the relief ordered.

The Court, having examined the Petition filed in this case and having conducted a hearing thereon, under oath, FINDS THAT:

❑ A. It has jurisdiction of the subject matter and over all necessary persons in these proceedings pursuant to:
    ❑ IDVA ❑ UCCJA

❑ B. _____ has/have been abused by Respondent, a family or household member
    as defined in the IDVA.

❑ C. Said abuse has consisted of:
    ❑ Physical abuse; ❑ Harassment; ❑ Interference with personal liberty; ❑ Intimidation of dependent; ❑ Willful deprivation

❑ D. The following persons are also protected by this Order:

    _____

    _____

❑ E. The Court has considered the nature, frequency, severity, pattern, and consequences of past abuse and the likelihood of future abuse
    to Petitioner or any member of Petitioner's or Respondent's family or household.

❑ F. For the remedy of Exclusive Possession of the Residence:
    ❑ Petitioner has a right to occupancy and Respondent has no right to occupancy;
    OR
    ❑ Both parties have a right to occupancy, and considering the risk of further abuse by Respondent interfering with Petitioner's safe
    and peaceful occupancy and all other relevant factors, the balance of hardships favors Petitioner.

❑ G. For the remedy relative to prohibitions on Respondent from entering or remaining present at Petitioner's school, place of
    employment, or their places at times when Petitioner is present:
    ❑ Respondent has no rights to enter/remain present at such place(s); or
    ❑ The balance of hardships favors Petitioner in prohibiting Respondent from entering or remaining at such place(s).
    ❑ The specific place(s) are as follows: _____.

❑ H. For the remedy of counseling, the likelihood of future abuse would be minimized by appropriate counseling services.

DOROTHY BROWN, CLERK OF THE CIRCUIT COURT OF COOK COUNTY, ILLINOIS

*Note: The Judge will complete this form if necessary.

SAMPLE 24 — CONTINUED

(This form replaces CCG-82-2)   (Rev. 4/7/03) CCDR 0802 B

☐ I. For the remedies of Temporary Legal Custody, Removal or Concealment of Child, Order to Appear, or Physical Care of Child, there exists a danger that a minor child will be (*Check applicable box(es)*):
☐ Abused or neglected;
☐ Improperly removed from this jurisdiction or improperly concealed within the State;
☐ Improperly separated from the child's primary caretaker.

☐ J. For the remedies of Temporary Legal Custody, Removal or Concealment of Child, Order to Appear, or Physical Care of Child,
_____ is or has been the primary caretaker of such minor child/ren.

☐ K. For the remedy of Exclusive Possession of Personal Property, as listed in the Petition:
☐ Petitioner, but not Respondent, owns such property.
OR
☐ Sharing the property creates a further risk of abuse or is impractical and the balance of hardships favors temporary possession by Petitioner, and
☐ Petitioner and Respondent own the property jointly, or
☐ The property is alleged to be marital property and a proceeding has been filed under the IMDMA.

☐ L. For the remedy of Protection of Property, as listed in the Petition:
☐ Petitioner, but not Respondent, owns such property.
OR
☐ The balance of hardships favors Petitioner, and
☐ Petitioner and Respondent own the property jointly, or
☐ The property is alleged to be marital property and a proceeding has been filed under the IMDMA.

☐ M. For the remedy of support, Respondent has a legal obligation to provide support to ☐ Petitioner and/or ☐ the minor child/ren.

☐ N. For the remedy of payment of losses, as a direct result of the abuse, the Petitioner has suffered the following losses:
_____
_____
_____

☐ O. For the remedy of Prohibition of Entry, Respondent constitutes a threat to the safety and well-being of Petitioner and/or Petitioner's child/ren by entering or remaining in the residence or household while under the influence of alcohol or drugs.

☐ P. For the remedy of surrender of any and all firearms, Respondent constitutes a threat to the safety of Petitioner and other protected parties by possession of said firearms. [Does not apply to Emergency Orders of Protection].

☐ Q. _____ is unable to bring the Petition on his/her own behalf due to age or disability.

☐ R. The disclosure of Petitioner's address would risk abuse of some member of the family or household or would reveal the confidential address of a shelter for domestic violence victims.

☐ S. [for Independent proceedings only] Filing fees are: ☐ Waived. ☐ Deferred.

☐ T. The hardship to Respondent, if remedy (ies) _____
is/are granted, substantially outweighs the hardship to Petitioner in the following manner: _____
_____
_____
_____

☐ U. Additional findings: _____
_____
_____
_____

DOROTHY BROWN, CLERK OF THE CIRCUIT COURT OF COOK COUNTY, ILLINOIS

Case No.: _____

FINDINGS: 3 of 3 Pages   (This form replaces CCG-82-2)   (Rev. 4/7/03) CCDR 0802 C

EMERGENCY ORDERS ONLY

☐ V.   For each of the remedies allowable under an Emergency Order of Protection, the harm which that remedy is intended to prevent would be likely to occur if Respondent were given any prior notice, or greater notice than was actually given, of Petitioner's efforts to obtain judicial relief.

☐ W.   For the remedy of Exclusive Possession of the Residence, the immediate danger of further abuse if Petitioner chooses or has chosen to remain in the residence or household, while Respondent was given any prior notice, or greater notice than was actually given, outweighs the hardship to Respondent.

☐ X.   For the remedy of Exclusive Possession of Personal Property, an improper disposition of the property would be likely to occur if Respondent were given any prior notice, or greater notice than was actually given, of Petitioner's efforts to obtain judicial relief, or Petitioner has an immediate and pressing need for possession of the property.

APPLICABLE TO ALL TYPES OF ORDERS

TRANSFERS, RESERVATIONS, OR DENIALS (which shall be set out in an order):

☐ I.   Requests for the following remedies are to be transferred by order to _____
as being a Court which ordinarily addresses such matters:

_____

_____

_____

☐ II.   Rulings on the following remedies are to be expressly reserved by this Court:

_____

_____

☐ III.   Relief with respect to the following remedies is to be denied for the following reasons:

_____

_____

_____

ENTER:

Dated: _____   _____

                                        Judge   Judge's No.

DOROTHY BROWN, CLERK OF THE CIRCUIT COURT OF COOK COUNTY, ILLINOIS

Case No.: _____

SAMPLE 25
APPLICANT TO SUE AS AN INDIGENT

3387 - Application to Sue or Defend as Indigent Person Petitioner - Allowed   4387 - Sue or Defend as Indigent - Allowed   4385 - Order Deferral of Fee Payment - Allowed
3487 - Application to Sue or Defend as Indigent Person Respondent - Allowed   5387 - Sue or Defend as Indigent Person - Denied
3388 - Application to Sue or Defend as Indigent Person Counter Petitioner - Allowed   4670 -Order Fees Waived - Allowed   (2/5/03) CCDR 0028 A

IN THE CIRCUIT COURT OF COOK COUNTY, ILLINOIS
COUNTY DEPARTMENT, DOMESTIC RELATIONS DIVISION

IN RE THE ☒ MARRIAGE ☐ CUSTODY ☐ SUPPORT OF:

Margaret Wood

PETITIONER

NO: _____

AND

Thomas Wood

CALENDAR: _____

RESPONDENT

APPLICATION, AFFIDAVIT AND ORDER TO SUE OR DEFEND AS AN INDIGENT PERSON

I, ___Margaret Wood___, age __41__ on oath state, ☒ On my own behalf, OR as ☐ Parent, ☐ Guardian,
(Petitioner/Respondent)

☐ Other _____ on behalf of _____ a(n) ☐ Minor OR ☐ Incompetent Adult;

1. ☒ I am the Petitioner and have a meritorious claim.
   ☐ I am the Respondent and have a meritorious defense.
   ☐ I am a Co-petitioner and have a meritorious claim.
2. I am unable to pay the cost of this case.
3. ☐ I am employed as a(n): _____ yearly gross salary $ _____
   (before taxes)

   Name of employer: _____

   Address of employer: _____ Telephone of employer: _____

4. ☒ I am unemployed as of __2/6/0-__, I began receiving Unemployment Compensation on __3/15/0-__
   in the amount of $ __500__ (per month)

5. ☒ My other sources of income are: ☐ SSI, ☒ Public Aid, ☐ Child Support, ☒ Food Stamps, ☐ Family Assistance, ☐ Foster care or
   ☐ Other: _____ $ _____ (per month)

6. The names and ages of persons dependent on the applicant for support are:
   __Emily Wood__ / __15__   _____ / _____   _____ / _____
   __Bradley Wood__ / __12__   _____ / _____   _____ / _____

7. The nature and value of property I own includes:
   Real Estate (describe property, specify address, present value and mortgage outstanding)
   __N/A__

   ☒ My Personal Property - consists of the following:
   ☒ Cash, bank accounts, etc. $ __200__, Clothing and jewelry $ __150__
   ☒ Furniture, appliances, household goods $ __600__
   ☐ Automobile - Model _____ Year _____ Value $ _____

8. During the past year, I have petitioned to sue or defend as an indigent person in the following matter(s):
   __N/A__

Name: __Margaret Wood__
Address: __1221 Evergreen Terrace__
City/State/Zip: __Anytown, IL 61121__
Telephone: __555-555-9817__
Firm/Business Name: __N/A__
Date: __5/29/0-__, _____

| Under penalties as provided by law pursuant to Section 1-109 of the Code of Civil Procedure, the undersigned certifies that the statements set forth in this instrument are true and correct, except as to matters therein stated to be on information and belief and as to such matters the undersigned certifies as aforesaid that s/he verily believes the same to be true. |

Margaret Wood
Signature of Applicant

ORDER
Pursuant to Supreme Court Rule 298 and 735 ILCS 5/5-105, it is hereby ordered:
4387 ☐ The applicant is permitted to sue without payment or fees, costs or charges.
   The applicant may be ordered to pay any portion of the waived fees or costs out of a settlement or judgment resulting from this action.

5387 ☐ The application is denied for the following reason(s): _____

4670 ☐ Payment shall be: ☐ made by _____ OR   4385 ☐ deferred until _____ OR ☐ other _____.

Date: _____, _____   Enter: _____
   Judge   Judge's No.

DOROTHY BROWN, CLERK OF THE CIRCUIT COURT OF COOK COUNTY, ILLINOIS

(2/5/03) CCDR 0028 B

735 ILCS 5/5-105.5

LEAVE TO SUE OR DEFEND AS AN INDIGENT PERSON (EFFECTIVE AUGUST 19, 1999)

(a) As used in this section:

(1) *"Fees, costs, and charges"* means payments imposed on a party in connection with the prosecution or defense of a civil action, including, but not limited to: filing fees; appearances fees; fees for service of process and other papers served either within or outside this State, including service by publication pursuant to Section 2-206 of this Code and publication of necessary legal notices; motion fees; jury demand fees; charges for participation in, or attendance at, any mandatory process or procedure including, but not limited to, conciliation, mediation, arbitration, counseling, evaluation, "Children First", "Focus on Children", or similar programs; fees for supplementary proceedings; charges for translation services; guardian ad litem fees; charges for certified copies of court documents; and all other processes and procedures deemed by the court to be necessary to commence, prosecute, defend, or enforce relief in a civil action.

2) *"Indigent person"* means any person who meets one or more of the following criteria:

(i) He or she is receiving assistance under one or more of the following public benefits programs: Supplemental Security Income (SSI), Aid to the Aged, Blind and Disabled (AABD), Temporary Assistance for Needy Families (TANF), Food Stamps, General Assistance, State Transitional Assistance, or State Children and Family Assistance.

(ii) His or her available income is 125% or less of the current poverty level as established by the United States Department of Health and Human Services, unless the applicant's assets that are not exempt under Part 9 or 10 of Article XII of this Code are of nature and value that the court determines that the applicant is able to pay the fees, costs and charges.

(iii) He or she is, in the discretion of the court, unable to proceed in an action without payment of fees, costs, and charges and whose payment of those fees, costs, and charges would result in substantial hardship to the person or his or her family.

(iv) He or she is an indigent person pursuant to Section 5-105.5 of this Code. [This states that "indigent person" means a person whose income is 125% or less of the current official federal poverty guidelines or who is otherwise eligible to receive civil legal services under the Legal Services Corporation Act of 1974. (42 U.S.CA. Sec. 2996 et. seq.)]

(b) On the application of any person, before or after the commencement of an action, a court, on finding that the applicant is an indigent person, shall grant the applicant leave to sue or defend the action without payment of the fees, costs and charges of the action.

(c) An application for leave to sue or defend an action as an indigent person shall be in writing and supported by the affidavit of the applicant or, if the applicant is a minor or an incompetent adult, by the affidavit of another person having knowledge of the facts. The contents of the affidavit shall be established by Supreme Court Rule.

(d) The court shall rule on applications under this Section in a timely manner based on information contained in the application unless the court, in its discretion, requires the applicant to personally appear to explain or clarify information contained in the application. If the court finds that the applicant is an indigent person, the court shall enter an order permitting the applicant to sue or defend without payment of fees, costs or charges. If the application is denied, the court shall enter an order to that effect stating the specific reasons for the denial. The clerk of the court shall promptly mail or deliver a copy of the order to the applicant.

(e) The clerk of the court shall not refuse to accept and file any complaint, appearance, or other paper presented by the applicant if accompanied by an application to sue or defend in forma pauperis, and those papers shall be considered filed on the date the application is presented. If the application is denied, the order shall state a date certain by which the necessary fees, costs, and charges must be paid. The court, for good cause shown, may allow an applicant whose application is denied to defer payment of fees, costs, and charges, make installment payments, or make payment upon reasonable terms and conditions stated in the order. The court may dismiss the claims or defenses of any party failing to pay the fees, costs, or charges within the time and in the manner ordered by the court. A determination concerning an application to sue or defend in forma pauperis shall not be construed as a ruling on the merits.

(f) The court may order an indigent person to pay all or a portion of the fees, costs, or charges waived pursuant to this Section out of monies recovered by the indigent person pursuant to a judgment or settlement resulting from the civil action. However, nothing in this Section shall be construed to limit the authority of a court to order another party to the action to pay the fees, costs, or charges of the action.

(g) A court, in its discretion, may appoint counsel to represent an indigent person, and that counsel shall perform his or her duties without fees, charges, or reward.

(h) Nothing in this Section shall be construed to affect the right of a party to sue or defend an action in forma pauperis without the payment of fees, costs, or charges, or the right of a party to court appointed counsel, as authorized by any other provision of law or by the rules of the Illinois Supreme Court.

(i) The provisions of this Section are severable under Section 1.31 the Statute on Statutes. See (5 ILCS 70/1.31)

DOROTHY BROWN, CLERK OF THE CIRCUIT COURT OF COOK COUNTY, ILLINOIS

APPENDIX

ILLINOIS CIRCUIT COURT CLERKS

Cook County Circuit

Cook County
Dorothy A. Brown
Richard J. Daley Center, Room 1001
Chicago, IL 60602-1305
Phone: 312-603-5030
Fax: 312-603-4557

First Judicial Circuit

Alexander County
Sharon McGinness
2000 Washington
Cairo, IL 62914-1717
Phone: 618-734-0107
Fax: 618-734-7003

Jackson County
Cindy R. Svanda
10th & Walnut
P.O. Box 730
Murphysboro, IL 62966-0730
Phone: 618-687-7300
Fax: 618-684-6378

Johnson County
Neal E. Watkins
Courthouse Square
P.O. Box 517
Vienna, IL 62995-0517
Phone: 618-658-4751
Fax: 618-658-2908

Massac County
Larry Grace
Superman Square, P.O. Box 152
Metropolis, IL 62960-1882
Phone: 618-524-5011
Fax: 618-524-4850

Pope County
Sean Goins
Main Street, P.O. Box 438
Golconda, IL 62938-0502
Phone: 618-683-3941
Fax: 618-683-3018

Pulaski County
Cindy Kennedy
N. 2nd & High Street, P.O. Box 88
Mound City, IL 62963-0088
Phone: 618-748-9300
Fax: 618-748-9329

Saline County
Jack T. Nolen
10 East Poplar
Harrisburg, IL 62946-1553
Phone: 618-253-5096
Fax: 618-253-3904

Union County
Lorraine Moreland
309 W. Market Street, Room 101
Jonesboro, IL 62952-0360
Phone: 618-833-5913
Fax: 618-833-5223

Williamson County
Stuart Hall
200 West Jefferson
Marion, IL 62959-2494
Phone: 618-997-1301
Fax: 618-998-9401

Second Judicial Circuit

Crawford County
Denise Utterback
Court Street, P.O. Box 655
Robinson, IL 62454-0655
Phone: 618-544-3512
Fax: 618-546-5628

Edwards County
Patsy Taylor
50 E. Main Street
Albion, IL 62806-1262
Phone: 618-445-2016
Fax: 618-445-4943

Franklin County
Donna Sevenski
On the Square, P.O. Box 485
Benton, IL 62812-2264
Phone: 618-439-2011
Fax: 618-439-4119

Gallatin County
Mona L. Moore
Lincoln Boulevard, P.O. Box 249
Shawneetown, IL 62984-0249
Phone: 618-269-3140
Fax: 618-269-4324

Hamilton County
Bobbi Oxford
Public Square
McLeansboro, IL 62859-1490
Phone: 618-643-3224
Fax: 618-643-3455

Hardin County
Diana Hubbard
Main & Market
P.O. Box 308
Elizabethtown, IL 62931-0308
Phone: 618-287-2735
Fax: 618-287-7833

Jefferson County
Gene Bolerjack
10th and Broadway, Box 1266
Mt. Vernon, IL 62864-1266
Phone: 618-244-8007
Fax: 618-244-8029

Lawrence County
Peggy Frederick
1100 State Street
Lawrenceville, IL 62439-2390
Phone: 618-943-2815
Fax: 618-943-5205

Richland County
Connie Kuenstler
103 West Main Street
Olney, IL 62450-2170
Phone: 618-392-2151
Fax: 618-392-8207

Wabash County
JoAnn Green
401 Market
P.O. Drawer 997
Mt. Carmel, IL 62863-1057
Phone: 618-262-5362
Fax: 618-263-4441

Wayne County
Sharon L. Gualdoni
301 East Main Street
P.O. Box 96
Fairfield, IL 62837-0096
Phone: 618-842-7684
Fax: 618-842-2556

White County
Ellen I. Pettijohn
301 East Main Street
P.O. Box 310
Carmi, IL 62821-0310
Phone: 618-382-2321
Fax: 618-382-2322

Third Judicial Circuit

Bond County
John K. King
200 West College
Greenville, IL 62246-1057
Phone: 618-664-3208
Fax: 618-664-4676

Madison County
Matt Melucci
155 N. Main
Edwardsville, IL 62025-1955
Phone: 618-692-6240
Fax: 618-692-0676

Fourth Judicial Circuit

Christian County
Donna Castelli
On the Square, Box 617
Taylorville, IL 62568-0617
Phone: 217-824-4966
Fax: 217-824-5105

Clay County
Rita L. Porter
On the Square, P.O. Box 100
Louisville, IL 62858-0100
Phone: 618-665-3523
Fax: 618-665-3543

Clinton County
Jeff Luebbers
850 Fairfax
Carlyle, IL 62231-0407
Phone: 618-594-2415
Fax: 618-594-0197

Effingham County
B. Jane Schuette
100 E. Jefferson, #101
P.O. Box 586
Effingham, IL 62401-0586
Phone: 217-342-4065
Fax: 217-342-6183

Fayette County
Marsha Wodtka
221 South Seventh
Vandalia, IL 62471-2755
Phone: 618-283-5009
Fax: 618-283-4490

Jasper County
Sheryl Frederick
100 West Jourdan
Newton, IL 62448-1973
Phone: 618-783-2524
Fax: 618-783-8626

Marion County
Ronda Yates
100 Main, P.O. Box 130
Salem, IL 62881-0130
Phone: 618-548-3856
Fax: 618-548-2358

Montgomery County
Mary Webb
120 N. Main Street, Box C
Hillsboro, IL 62049-0210
Phone: 217-532-9546
Fax: 217-532-9519

Shelby County
Cheryl Roley
P.O. Box 469
Shelbyville, IL 62565-0469
Phone: 217-774-4212
Fax: 217-774-4109

Fifth Judicial Circuit

Clark County
Terri Reynolds
501 Archer Avenue, Box 187
Marshall, IL 62441-0187
Phone: 217-826-2811
Fax: 217-826-1396

Coles County
Vicki Kirkpatrick
6th and Jackson, Box 48
Charleston, IL 61920-0048
Phone: 217-348-0516
Fax: 217-348-7324

Cumberland County
Tina Gabel
Courthouse Square, Box 145
Toledo, IL 62468-0145
Phone: 217-849-3601
Fax: 217-849-3183

Edgar County
Janis K. Nebergall
115 West Court St.
Paris, IL 61944-1739
Phone: 217-466-7447
Fax: 217-466-7443

Vermilion County
Susan Miller
7 North Vermilion Street
Danville, IL 61832-5806
Phone: 217-431-2541
Fax: 217-431-2538

Sixth Judicial Circuit

Champaign County
Linda S. Frank
101 East Main Street
Urbana, IL 61801-2736
Phone: 217-384-3725
Fax: 217-384-3879

DeWitt County
Kathy A. Weiss
201 W. Washington Street
Clinton, IL 61727-0439
Phone: 217-935-2195
Fax: 217-935-3310

Douglas County
Julie Mills
401 South Center, P.O. Box 50
Tuscola, IL 61953-0050
Phone: 217-253-2352
Fax: 217-253-9006

Macon County
Kathy Hott
253 East Wood Street
Decatur, IL 62523-1489
Phone: 217-424-1454
Fax: 217-424-1350

Moultrie County
Deborah M. Preston
10 South Main Street
Sullivan, IL 61951-1969
Phone: 217-728-4622
Fax: 217-728-7833

Piatt County
Gary Bickel
101 W. Washington Street
Monticello, IL 61856-0288
Phone: 217-762-4966
Fax: 217-762-8394

Seventh Judicial Circuit

Greene County
V. "Tunie" Brannan
519 North Main Street
Carrollton, IL 62016-1093
Phone: 217-942-3421
Fax: 217-942-5431

Jersey County
Charles E. Huebener
201 West Pearl
Jerseyville, IL 62052-1852
Phone: 618-498-5571
Fax: 618-498-6128

Macoupin County
Mike Mathis
201 East Main Street
Carlinville, IL 62626-1824
Phone: 217-854-3211
Fax: 217-854-8561

Morgan County
Theresa Lonergan
300 West State Street, Box 1120
Jacksonville, IL 62650-1165
Phone: 217-243-5419
Fax: 217-243-2009

Sangamon County
Anthony P. Libri
200 South 9th Street, Room 405
Springfield, IL 62701-1299
Phone: 217-753-6674
Fax: 217-753-6665

Scott County
Joni Garrett
35 East Market Street
Winchester, IL 62694-1216
Phone: 217-742-5217
Fax: 217-742-5853

Eighth Judicial Circuit

Adams County
Glen F. Hultz
521 Vermont Street
Quincy, IL 62301-2934
Phone: 217-277-2100
Fax: 217-277-2116

Brown County
Doris Todd
#1 Court Street
Mt. Sterling, IL 62353-1233
Phone: 217-773-2713
Fax: 217-773-2233

Calhoun County
Yvonne Macauley
Main & County Roads
Hardin, IL 62047-0486
Phone: 618-576-2451
Fax: 618-576-9541

Cass County
Evelyn K. Trenter
P.O. Box 203
Virginia, IL 62691-0203
Phone: 217-452-7225
Fax: 217-452-7219

Mason County
Brenda Miller
125 N. Plum
Havana, IL 62644-0377
Phone: 309-543-6619
Fax: 309-543-4214

Menard County
Penny Hoke
P.O. Box 466
Petersburg, IL 62675-0466
Phone: 217-632-2615
Fax: 217-632-4124

Pike County
Ben Johnson
100 East Washington
Pittsfield, IL 62363-1497
Phone: 217-285-6612
Fax: 217-285-4726

Schuyler County
Elaine Boyd
Lafayette & Congress, P.O. Box 80
Rushville, IL 62681-0189
Phone: 217-322-4633
Fax: 217-322-6164

Ninth Judicial Circuit

Fulton County
Mary C. Hampton
100 North Main Street
P.O. Box 152
Lewistown, IL 61542-0152
Phone: 309-547-3041
Fax: 309-547-3674

Hancock County
John Neally
Courthouse Square, Box 189
Carthage, IL 62321-0189
Phone: 217-357-2616
Fax: 217-357-2231

Henderson County
Sandra D. Keane
4th & Warren
Box 546
Oquawka, IL 61469-0546
Phone: 309-867-3121
Fax: 309-867-3207

Knox County
Kelly A. Cheesman
200 South Cherry Street
Galesburg, IL 61401-4912
Phone: 309-343-3121
Fax: 309-343-7002

McDonough County
Julia A. Vestal
#1 Courthouse Square
P.O. Box 348
Macomb, IL 61455-0348
Phone: 309-837-4889
Fax: 309-833-4493

Warren County
Jill M. Morris
100 West Broadway
Monmouth, IL 61462-1795
Phone: 309-734-5179
Fax: 309-734-4151

Tenth Judicial Circuit

Marshall County
Gina M. Noe
122 N. Prairie, P.O. Box 328
Lacon, IL 61540-0328
Phone: 309-246-6435
Fax: 309-246-2173

Peoria County
Robert Spears
324 Main Street, Room G22
Peoria, IL 61602-1319
Phone: 309-672-6989
Fax: 309-677-6228

Putnam County
Cathy J. Oliveri
120 North 4th Street
Hennepin, IL 61327-0207
Phone: 815-925-7016
Fax: 815-925-7549

Stark County
Marian E. Purtscher
130 Main Street, Box 426
Toulon, IL 61483-0426
Phone: 309-286-5941
Fax: 309-286-4039

Tazewell County
Pamela J. Gardner
342 Court Street
Pekin, IL 61554-0069
Phone: 309-477-2214
Fax: 309-353-7801

Eleventh Judicial Circuit

Ford County
Kamalen K. Johnson
200 West State, Box 80
Paxton, IL 60957-0080
Phone: 217-379-2641
Fax: 217-379-3445

Livingston County
Judith K. Cremer
112 West Madison Street
Pontiac, IL 61764-0320
Phone: 815-844-2602
Fax: 815-842-1844

Logan County
Carla Bender
601 Broadway, P.O. Box 158
Lincoln, IL 62656-0158
Phone: 217-735-2376
Fax: 217-732-1231

McLean County
Sandra K. Parker
104 West Front Street, Room 404
Bloomington, IL 61702-2400
Phone: 309-888-5324
Fax: 309-888-5281

Woodford County
Carol J. Newtson
115 North Main Street
P.O. Box 284
Eureka, IL 61530-0284
Phone: 309-467-3312
Fax: 309-467-4626

Twelfth Judicial Circuit

Will County
Pamela J. McGuire
14 West Jefferson Street
Joliet, IL 60432-4399
Phone: 815-727-8585
Fax: 815-727-8896

Thirteenth Judicial Circuit

Bureau County
Michael L. Miroux
702 South Main Street
Princeton, IL 61356-2037
Phone: 815-872-2001
Fax: 815-872-0027

Grundy County
Karen Slattery
111 E. Washington Street, Room 30
Morris, IL 60450-0707
Phone: 815-941-3258
Fax: 815-942-2222

LaSalle County
Joseph Carey
119 W. Madison
Ottawa, IL 61350-0617
Phone: 815-434-8671
Fax: 815-433-9198

Fourteenth Judicial Circuit

Henry County
Debra J. Doss
307 West Center Street
P.O. Box 9
Cambridge, IL 61238-0009
Phone: 309-937-3572
Fax: 309-937-3990

Mercer County
Jeff G. Benson
100 Southeast 3rd Street, P.O. Box 175
Aledo, IL 61231-0175
Phone: 309-582-7122
Fax: 309-582-7121

Rock Island County
Lisa L. Bierman
210 15th Street, Box 5230
Rock Island, IL 61201-5230
Phone: 309-786-4451
Fax: 309-786-3029

Whiteside County
Jane Fransen
200 East Knox Street
Morrison, IL 61270-2819
Phone: 815-772-5188
Fax: 815-772-5187

Fifteenth Judicial Circuit

Carroll County
Sherri A. Miller
301 North Main Street
Mt. Carroll, IL 61053-0032
Phone: 815-244-0230
Fax: 815-244-3869

Jo Daviess County
Sharon A. Wand
330 North Bench Street
Galena, IL 61036-1828
Phone: 815-777-0037
Fax: 815-777-2229

Lee County
Denise A. McCaffrey
309 S. Galena, Box 325
Dixon, IL 61021-0325
Phone: 815-284-5234
Fax: 815-288-5615

Ogle County
Martin W. Typer
4th & Washington
Oregon, IL 61061-0337
Phone: 815-732-3201
Fax: 815-732-6273

Stephenson County
Bonnie K. Curran
15 North Galena Street
Freeport, IL 61032-0785
Phone: 815-235-8266
Fax: 815-233-1576

Sixteenth Judicial Circuit

DeKalb County
Maureen Josh
133 West State Street
Sycamore, IL 60178-1416
Phone: 815-895-7131
Fax: 815-895-7140

Kane County
Deborah Seyller
540 S. Randall Rd.
St. Charles, IL 60174
Phone: 630-232-3413
Fax: 630-208-2172

Kendall County
Shirley R. Lee
807 W. John Street, P.O. Box M
Yorkville, IL 60560-0259
Phone: 630-553-4183
Fax: 630-553-4964

Seventeenth Judicial Circuit

Boone County
Julie Kleive
601 North Main, #303
Belvidere, IL 61008-2644
Phone: 815-544-0371
Fax: 815-547-9213

Winnebago County
Marc A. Gasparini
400 West State Street
Rockford, IL 61101-1221
Phone: 815-987-5464
Fax: 815-987-3012

Eighteenth Judicial Circuit

DuPage County
Joel Kagann
505 N. County Farm Road
Wheaton, IL 60189-0707
Phone: 630-682-7111
Fax: 630-682-7085

Nineteenth Judicial Circuit

Lake County
Sally D. Coffelt
18 North County Street
Waukegan, IL 60085-4340
Phone: 847-377-3380
Fax: 847-360-6409

McHenry County
Vernon W. Kays
2200 North Seminary Avenue
Woodstock, IL 60098-2837
Phone: 815-334-4000
Fax: 815-338-8583

Twentieth Judicial Circuit

Monroe County
Aaron Reitz
100 South Main Street
Waterloo, IL 62298-1322
Phone: 618-939-8681
Fax: 618-939-5132

Perry County
Nick Dolce
Courthouse Square, Box 219
Pinckneyville, IL 62274-0219
Phone: 618-357-6726
Fax: 618-357-3923

Randolph County
Barbara Brown
#1 Taylor Street
Chester, IL 62233-0329
Phone: 618-826-3116
Fax: 618-826-3750

St. Clair County
C. Barney Metz
10 Public Square
Belleville, IL 62220-1623
Phone: 618-277-6832
Fax: 618-277-1925

Washington County
Carol Heggemeier
101 E. St. Louis Street
Nashville, IL 62263-1100
Phone: 618-327-4800
Fax: 618-327-3583

Twenty-First Judicial Circuit

Iroquois County
Arlene J. Hines
550 South Tenth Street
Watseka, IL 60970-1810
Phone: 815-432-6950
Fax: 815-432-0347

Kankakee County
Kathryn Thomas
450 East Court Street
Kankakee, IL 60901-3917
Phone: 815-937-2905
Fax: 815-937-3903

GLOSSARY

AFFIDAVIT

A written statement made voluntarily and under oath and witnessed by a notary public

ANNULMENT

The termination of an illegal marriage

CASE NUMBER

A number that is placed on the Petition when it is filed and used on all other papers filed in the same action

CERTIFIED COPY

A copy of something that the circuit court clerk has placed a seal on and declared the same as the original in the court file

CIRCUIT COURT CLERK

An elected public official who keeps the court records and with whom divorce papers are filed

COMMINGLED

Mixed together; used to describe property when it's impossible to tell what's marital property and what's non-marital property (when property is commingled, courts treat it all as marital property)

COMMUNITY PROPERTY STATE

States in which all property acquired during the marriage is owned jointly by husband and wife, regardless of whose money was used to acquire the property. The nine community property states are Arizona, California, Idaho, Louisiana, Nevada, New Mexico, Texas, Washington State, and Wisconsin.

CONTEMPT OF COURT

The failure to do something the court has ordered

CONTESTED DIVORCE

When spouses are deadlocked about one or more aspects of the divorce process and cannot come to an agreement on their own

DEFAULT

When the respondent fails to respond to the Petition or otherwise respond as required by law

INDIGENT

Unable to afford court costs and/or an attorney

INJUNCTION

A paper signed by a judge or court commissioner that prohibits a person from doing something or orders a person to do something

INSTANTER

Immediately, right away. A judge who grants a Judgment of Dissolution *instanter* will sign it at the hearing, making the divorce immediately final.

JUDGMENT OF DISSOLUTION

The document signed by the judge that officially ends your marriage

LAWS OF SUCCESSION

The laws that govern how your property is divided among your heirs after you die

MAINTENANCE

The money paid by one spouse to another after a divorce; formerly called *alimony*

MARITAL PROPERTY

Property that is acquired after marriage and considered jointly owned by both spouses

MOTION

A request to the court asking that something be done, such as withholding income for support

NOTARY PUBLIC

A public official who is authorized to administer oaths and swear that signatures are authentic

OATH

To make a statement in which one promises, under penalty of law, to tell the truth to the judge or court official

PETITION

The form requesting a dissolution of marriage; it is filed at the circuit court clerk's office

PETITIONER

The person asking the court for a dissolution of marriage

PRENUPTIAL AGREEMENT

An agreement signed before marriage that limits the rights of one or both parties with respect to the property of the other

PRO SE

A Latin term meaning "for the self"; in this context, it means you are representing yourself without an attorney

PROVE-UP

Another name for the hearing in front of the judge, so called because you and your spouse are required to prove the facts you've alleged in your Petition

RESPONDENT

The spouse who is not filing the Petition of Dissolution

RESTRAINING ORDER

See *Injunction*

VERIFIED FORMS

Forms that are signed under oath in front of a notary public